"Sam Serio has written the book that few others would have. In a sensitive manner, and with absolute care not to offend, he explains how to preach from most of the biblical passages dealing with sexual sin. You will receive much help from his frequent tips. I know of no other book like it. You will want a copy."

—Jay E. Adams,
founder of The Institute for Nouthetic Studies

"Finally—a powerful tool for pastors and counselors. Dr. Serio shares his profound knowledge of Scripture and sexual abuse throughout this book. Those who wish to address the walking wounded from sexual sins, but don't know how, will find this a phenomenal resource. Sam Serio's book should be in every pastor's study and every Christian counselor's office. I especially like the final chapter, 'My Challenge to the Church of the Future.' Through counseling, marriage preparation, and sermons, we absolutely *must* address the issue of abnormal sexuality and its consequences. *Everyone* is affected by the topics discussed in this amazing book."

—Karen (Austin) McDonald,
counselor and president of Racheal's Rest

"Dr. Sam Serio's wisdom comes from years of research into and experience dealing with tough topics. As a survivor of sexual abuse, I can personally say the chapter on sexual abuse is not only brilliant but much needed. I can't adequately describe the pain, confusion, and rejection I felt during my early years in recovery when I tried to attain support and direction for healing from the leadership in my church. Dr. Serio has a passion for empowering pastors to address the pain, sin, and bondage inherent in sexual deviance and to apply the Word of God to heal their flocks."

—Tammy Kennedy,
founder of The King's Treasure Box Ministries

SENSITIVE PREACHING
TO THE SEXUALLY HURTING

DR. SAM SERIO

Kregel
Ministry

Sensitive Preaching to the Sexually Hurting
© 2016 by Sam Serio

Published by Kregel Publications, a division of Kregel, Inc., 2450 Oak
Industrial Dr. NE, Grand Rapids, MI 49505-6020.

ISBN 978-0-8254-4417-3

Printed in the United States of America
16 17 18 19 20 / 5 4 3 2 1

CONTENTS

PREPARING YOUR HEART
AND YOUR CHURCH

1

WHO'S IN YOUR PEWS?

Did you know that the teenage couple sitting in the front seat of your church on Sunday morning is having sex in the back seat of their car on Saturday night?

Meanwhile, the middle-aged couple sitting behind them have not had sex in in the last year, are having serious marital issues, and are already talking of divorce.

One of your ushers wasn't there Sunday morning because he stayed up too late on Saturday night clicking on those porn sites he just can't get enough of.

Your choir director missed this past Mother's Day service because she didn't want to be reminded about the abortion she had.

Betty never attends the Father's Day service because she doesn't want to be reminded to "honor and obey" the man who sexually molested her for years.

Susie always misses the evening service because she doesn't want to leave the house at night now—ever since she was raped one night behind a nearby convenience store.

Wayne always misses the men's monthly breakfast because he doesn't feel comfortable around men who don't know his struggles with homosexuality.

Mary lost her interest in missionary work about the same time she lost her baby in the abortion. She remembers your sermons about how God hates abortion and fornication. She gave up hope that God could ever use her in world missions.

Rod also remembers your sermons about how much God hates homosexuality. That's why he tried to commit suicide, but no one will know that—especially you!

Carole continues to silently struggle over her middle-age miscarriage because she thinks God is still punishing her for her teenage promiscuity.

Janet's husband doesn't know how terrified she is to have sex with him ever since her boss raped her at work. She is scared of giving AIDS to her husband, losing her job, or losing her husband who would want to kill her boss if he knew what happened.

Molly struggles because she waited her whole life as a virgin for her husband, only to be miserable now that he has no interest in sex with her and snores while she cries at night.

And don't be too quick to judge Mrs. Jones for wanting a divorce! Ask her about her husband's forcing her to act out the sexual positions and perversions he sees on the sites. He expects the same from her and now, she wants to leave.

And please don't get mad at Melissa who is now distant and devastated upon hearing that her husband wants to leave her and proudly live that gay life that he has secretly had for twenty years now.

Tim's parents just can't understand why he seems so distant and quiet now. After he told them that his gym teacher tried to touch him, they told him to stop making up silly stories and just be quiet. So, now he *is* quiet.

Michelle and her daughter are also quiet. They refuse to go back to the house ever since she caught her husband sexually fondling their daughter while tucking her into bed last night. Meanwhile, the church ladies continue to gossip about Michelle.

Lilly won't volunteer for helping out in the church nursery. She's really uncomfortable around children because they remind her of the baby she aborted. She can't help wondering which one would have looked just like hers.

But that's okay, since Tom fills in every Sunday! He loves to be around little children since they remind him of the ones he sees in his secret movies at night.

Little Amy is one of those children. Bet you didn't know that the reason she runs away from you every time you kindly offer her candy at church is because that's exactly what "Teacher Tom" offered her before he touched her privates.

Did you know how horrible Angie feels from being continuously told her entire married life that she is not woman enough—only to later discover her husband was only interested in men? Years of daily degradation have taken their toll. She didn't have a chance, no matter how hard she tried to please him.

Did you know that your deacon resigned so he could spend more time with his family? His son announced that he was gay. They'll never tell you that family news because they know how you feel about homosexuals. They hear your sermons.

Did you know that Paula, your most zealous pro-lifer at church, is desperately trying to prove to God how truly sorry she is for having that abortion in the past?

Did you know that Sheila, who pickets the pornographic stores, is trying to erase her childhood memories of having to watch similar movies with her Dad?

Did you know that your newest church member happens to also be a lesbian? She was gang-raped in high school after her graduation party and that's why she now prefers women over men. She'll keep all of this a secret.

Katie was date-raped in college, and now freezes up and gives excuses as she refuses her husband who wants to be intimate with her at night. He feels so rejected by her and had no idea that marriage with Katie would be so difficult.

No one knows why shy little Sally doesn't come to youth group events. Her dad limits her social activities at church because of his sexual activities at home.

No—this is not the daily digest of reality TV, Facebook post-ings, lunchroom gossip, late night TV, or daytime soap operas. This is real life. These are the people in your pews, chairs, and churches on Sunday mornings. You'd be amazed at how many people in your church are either sexually wounded, hurting, struggling, addicted, tempted, or devastated, but will never tell you. It's a whole lot more than you could ever imagine. They have severe sexual pain in their memories or in their families. If not found directly in them, then it is in their children or grand-children's families. Rarely is there any family without sexual sadness and skeletons hidden in their closets. Everybody has that one chapter they don't read out loud.

It's time for the church to open our eyes not only to the harvest, but also to the wreckage!

They are the casualties of the sexual revolution that's been going on for years. Whenever there is a war or a revolution, there is a mess. A lot of people have been left limping. They are the walking wounded. Many are dazed and confused—not having a clue on where to get help. They wonder what hit them and they don't know how to recover. They're hesitant to share what has been done to them or by them. They suffer in silence, they sin in secret. These casualties of the sexual revolution come in all shapes and sizes, genders and ages. They're in the world but they're also in your church—either as members, seekers, attenders, volunteers, or leaders. They sit in your church with superficial smiles, monstrous memories, hidden hurts, mixed motives, and agonizing addictions. They stand a few feet away from the hidden key that could finally set them free: you! As their preacher and pastor who best knows God's Word, *you have the solution* they need—but they're usually not coming to you for that answer.

Here's why:

We can be rather insensitive or incompetent. We tend to neglect either truth or grace in sermons about sex. In Jesus' name, we can fail miserably whenever we preach about sex.

> *Open our eyes to the fact that sexually wounded or addicted people don't or won't come to you for their healing because of how you preach.*

Most ministry leaders usually do one of two things when it comes to this kind of delicate preaching on these most difficult topics—we are either negligent or negative. We either say nothing, or we say mean things. We ignore, or we abhor. There is rarely a happy medium. Which extreme are you most likely to do? When is the last time you mentioned something about sex? And if you did approach this subject, how did you sound? Is your preaching about sex easily summed up with a bunch of Bible verses mentioning God's wrath? Or did you maybe do the opposite, and only talk about God's love but not about God's law? Do you have that rare biblical balance? Do you preach truth and grace? Do you preach love and law? Facts and feelings? Proclamation and consolation? When is the last time you actually smiled as you preached about sex and offered hope and restoration, healing and wholeness, forgiveness and transformation?

That is the purpose of this book.

*Seminary probably didn't prepare you for the sexual issues
we face.* They didn't offer you much in their curriculum about
how to effectively counsel or preach to a sexually wounded
and addicted generation, did they? It was too taboo and controversial. They didn't do it then and they still aren't doing it
today. Yet they claim that they're preparing the leaders of the
next generation for Christ? *Not.* They have failed to keep up
with the sexual topics which God has addressed. I estimate that
sixty to eighty percent of all adults (sixteen years or older) in
our churches are emotionally affected by sexual pain or sin that
has been done by them or to them. This is no small matter or
minority in our churches, and it must be taught in seminaries.

You preach to a generation who believes that it is more
important to recycle than it is to abstain from porn. You preach
to women who have been raped. You preach to men who are
secret and serial rapists. Some have actually molested small
children. And some of your members were molested when they
were small children. Some women had an abortion. Some men
insisted on their baby being aborted. You preach to a generation who believes that sex is meant to express yourself, demonstrate intimacy with someone you think you love, fulfill your
needs, or to connect with another person in an enjoyable way.
Gen-Xers, Boomers and Millennials reject the biblical notion
that sex is meant by God to unite a man and a woman in marriage. We have an uphill battle, since there has been an immense cultural shift! Some of your church members are gay
or lesbian. Some are porn addicts and their wives feel inferior.
Some marriages are on the brink of divorce because of a lack
of sexual intimacy. Some of your church members have various
sexual partners or complicated sexual struggles. This is the real
generation of people to whom you are now ministering.

Did you ever consider the fact that church is one of the very
best places to hide your sin and cover up your lifestyle? People
assume you're right with God because you're sitting in church.
No one asks you about your Saturday night walk with God because of your Sunday morning seat at church! And then, we all
act so shocked when we hear of church members/attenders who
were actively engaged in some scandalous sin and we wonder
how this could have happened! You're trusted, you're validated

and you've got the best cover at church. That is what some of my counseling clients have secretly told me in their disclosure. Don't be naive to think that your church is automatically immune and free from sexual predators. Don't forget this important truth that God already included in His Word (Jer. 9:2–6; 23:9–11; Matt. 7:15; Acts 20:29–31; Jude 1:4).

What sermons did you preach to comfort rape victims or to confront rapists? What have you done to publicly or privately heal your church members who were molested as children? How can the woman who had an abortion get release from her guilt? Have your sermons taught men how to get victory over addiction to porn? What do you say to the homosexuals who are willing to change? Do you talk about sex in marriage being a gift from God that is not to be withheld by either spouse? Do you assume that all the weddings you perform happen to consist of virgins?

Some of your people need to be convicted, while some need to be consoled. Which is easiest for you to do? Rare is the preacher who can seamlessly do both. Which emotions are you most inclined to preach? Are you usually too easy or too hard on people when it comes to everyday sin and especially our sexual sin? Don't answer too quickly and don't assume you preach both with the same effectiveness. Might your theology be one-sided and imbalanced in this? Most preaching about sex is either antinomian or antagonistic. Either God's law or God's love is not communicated effectively today. Can you actually preach both messages of conviction and consolation? Better yet, can you preach each of these in the same sermon? Can you change your tempo? This book will help you.

When you finally do decide to preach about sex, remember that this is not about a topic nor is this about an issue. It's, instead, all about individuals! That premise will change your preaching. You're not ever preaching about sex as a topic or an issue; you are preaching *to people* who are sexually wounded or sexually addicted. They have sexual hurts and habits. They have dark secrets and deep trauma. When you preach about sex, your purpose is not to expound—your purpose is to expose this sexual pain or sin. You're there to do surgery, not give a soliloquy. You're changing the lives of sexual victims and victimizers—from your sermon! The deepest healing for sexual hurt or habits comes from God's Word, not from a man's advice in an office or a therapist. We have a God who has all-sufficient grace for all sexual hurt. He has immeasurable power for people who have sexual memories or temptations that are beyond their power. Healing can come from a preacher. Why do sexually hurt people go to the world and not to the preacher for help? Why are pastors the last people on earth they would ever consider coming to for help? Is this possibly our own fault?

Here's a question to ask ourselves:

Do I publicly communicate about sex in such a way that people would want to come to me for additional counseling afterward OR do I preach in such a way that they would not want to come to me for counseling after they just heard what I said and also how I said it on a typical Sunday?

Let me help you answer that initial question by posing another question for you. How many people *are* currently and continually coming to you (or coming to your designated or specialized staff members) for some type of sexual help or private counseling right now? How few? Be honest. Might there be a correlation or connection? Why might they not be coming?

I can't tell you the countless number of people who have told me they would *never* approach their pastor or priest for personal counseling after they heard his or her preaching on any topics surrounding sex. Who wants to get yelled at again? They already feel horrible inside and now they honestly believe they will feel worse—because of you. You have not shown much truth or grace and as a result, you might have turned people away in your sermons. Maybe the opposite is true, though. Maybe, some feel far too comfortable and smug in their sin, because of you. As George Whitefield once said, "It is a poor sermon that gives no offense that neither makes the hearer displeased with himself nor with the preacher." Do you think that is the furthest thing from the truth or do you think that is accurate? Might there be a middle ground? Others tell me how their church just does not discuss anything about sex. You have preached no conviction of sin and personally believe their selfish sexual behavior merits no mention from the pulpit. I'm trying to cover the wide range of our belief systems and preaching styles.

Whenever you do mention any sexual topics from the pulpit, do you genuinely communicate warmth or tenderness?

How so? Are your arms extended or are your fists clenched or fingers pointed? Do you smile as you look into their eyes when you are inviting people to give their agony or addiction to God who can help them the most? A pew is better than a podcast; you can communicate better to your people, who need to see your face. Would a teenager or family in the church with an unplanned pregnancy ever come to you for help, based on how you regularly preach about sex? Do people think you are truly conversational and approachable, or would they avoid you like the plague in terms of sexual topics? Do people in your church think that you're an expert on sex, or that you're way over your head on this one?

The purpose of this book is to help you communicate both warmth and wisdom when it comes to any and every topic relating to sexuality. That's what God does.

This book will help you improve both your preaching and counseling ministries to sexually confused or consumed people who happen to be all around you today. This is the book you should give to all the members of your staff who specialize in ministry to women, men, couples, marriages, counseling, young adults, teenagers or children in your church. They need this book, too.

Mother Teresa once said, "You can see Calcutta all over the world if you have eyes to see."

That's my goal here. I want you to have the eyes to see and the words to say. I want to help you become the expert you are supposed to be in the topic of sex. Sex begins in the church—not in the kitchen or the bedroom. Here is where we should get our education, not there. There is so much to learn when it comes to seeing how God's Word is so sufficient. There is so much to learn about helping others and also yourself! You'll experience depths of depression that you never deemed possible, as you listen. You'll never forget some of their stories. They will haunt you. They will leave you a different person. Outrage and shock, tenderness and compassion—these deep emotions will come out in full intensity. You'll want to cry, and you'll want others to pay for what they did! You'll have to learn to control your anger as you confront people who have selfishly and sexually damaged others and who have taken advantage of their childhood innocence. Can you handle your emotions while talking to the adult who has abused or molested a child? Can you restore the marriage destroyed by porn? By sexual reluctance? Do you know what to say to the spouse who has been brought to ruin by their spouse, who has cheated with someone of the opposite or the same sex? Can you control your emotions and words? Can you act just like Jesus in this situation?

This book will show you why people actually commit sexual sin and why people are totally devastated as a result of that sexual sin. You can help both.

This revolutionary book deals with a wide variety of sexual hurts or habits from a preaching perspective.

You'll be fully equipped on what to say and how best to say it. You'll get the specific pre-packaged words you can carefully use in your own sermons as you console or confront people. You'll learn how to apply a wide variety of Bible characters, texts, and stories. You'll learn to creatively and deeply minister to people whose lives have been truly shattered by sexual sin or pain. It took many hours to carefully craft the transitions and segues in each sermon as I carefully chose certain words that accurately move you from the text to the application. I hope you will use these words which have been tested and proven in a variety of settings, public and private! You'll gain a greater confidence in the power of God's Word. You'll see God's Spirit bring conviction—and consolation—in ways in which you have never dreamed. You'll be amazed at how God brings sexual healing to all the brokenhearted, and sexual freedom to the captives. *He is the solution for any and all kinds of hurts or habits, including sexual ones which we consider to be off-limits for Christians.* That is the premise for this book. He *is* the God of hope (Rom. 15:13) and God of comfort (2 Cor. 1:3–4) who is able to make all things new (2 Cor. 5:17) and who makes all kinds of people brand new (Rev. 21:5). There is no emotional or sexual pain or sin in this world that lies beyond God's transforming and healing grace. None.

2

ARE YOU AND YOUR CHURCH READY FOR THIS MINISTRY?

If you want to have a public and private ministry to the sexually wounded and addicted in your church and community ... beware *and* prepare! Yes, the fields are ripe unto harvest, but they're also filled with explosive landmines that can destroy your ministry, family, and future. Walk very carefully and slowly as you embark. Be extremely patient, because this will take time. This kind of ministry *should* not happen overnight and *will* not happen overnight. You will need to get some things in order. Both you and your church will need to change some key concepts you currently have about God, the church, the worship service, and your limitations.

There are some major myths and misconceptions about the church and the pastor that will also need to be changed if you're going to minister in this arena. Since you're the pastor, you'll hopefully be that main change agent. You'll need to gradually and patiently re-educate your church members about sin and sex.

Let's examine seven biblical truths you'll need to firmly believe and wisely communicate:

1. **Church is the best—not the worst—place to go for our sexual healing.**

People wrongly think that the church is the *last place* you go to for help about sex. The world also thinks that the preacher or pastor is the *last person* you go to for expertise in sexual matters. People are told to go to the therapist, the analyst, the specialist, the doctor, the counseling center, or anywhere else *but* the pastor or preacher of a church. How sad that such a myth exists! Most people erroneously believe that you especially ought not to wade in the sexual waters that should be reserved for the "professionals." You will be told that quite often. Watch and see.

In order to minister in the future, you must try to reverse this popular pagan thinking about who best can help the victims of the ongoing sexual revolution. The world can't, but the church can—and you can—because God can heal and give hope. He is the Great Physician. He breaks the power of dwelling sin and changes the belief systems and daily habits of sinners. We just express our sin differently. *Bible teachers should be the best equipped and the most skilled types of sexual counselors, analysts, therapists, and specialists.* Do you believe that? I hope so. His Word is the best tool to train people in righteousness so that they are thoroughly equipped for every good work. Churches are the best local hospitals for the sexually wounded or addicted. Here is the place where sexually broken people should get the very best care, diagnosis, and treatment for what consumes them! God teaches us that sanctification happens best when we're around the best of people, which are God's people. In spite of all our flaws, we are the best hospital. We let the world take sex away from the church but it is God who created sex; if anyone knows best about sex, it is Him. God doesn't want His people to go over to Egypt and the world for help (Isa. 31:1) when they should be going to Him.

2. Church should be up*lifting*, but it doesn't have to be up*beat*.

There is a difference in the details. We have somehow gotten the wrong notion that church has to always conclude on a positive enthusiastic note, where everybody leaves with smiling faces and happy handshakes. We think the pastor is paid to make us feel energized and enthused and be a glorified cheerleader to the congregation. Positivity is the new politically correct but spiritually incorrect word. Are people supposed to leave with a smile but go home and cry? They do. People wrongly think that the church should *never* be somber, but it can be. God is holy, and sometimes a holy hush or godly silence can be a very good way to end church. Crying is good if the Spirit of God so leads. There are so many people who need to grieve and weep. Are they allowed or encouraged to, as your sermon or service comes to a close?

Church is supposed to make us
be good, not just feel good!

As long as you and your members believe that your job is to make people smile big and feel good, you will never have an effective preaching ministry to the sexually wounded. Touching a nerve, convicting a conscience, or opening a wound is all good with God. Surgery is painful and you don't wake up with a big smile at first. It may not feel or look good but it is. It is perfectly fine to have rivers of tears, loud wailing, and intense crying during a church service if God is in the midst of mending some broken hearts. What is wrong with people coming to the front for prayer because they are overcome with grief for how they have sexually hurt others in the past? If some of your members get upset—because the church is now getting far too emotional, because you are preaching to their innermost hurts—it's okay. Let some whine, but let others weep.

Jesus is the Great Physician, not the Great Cheerleader or the Great Clown! The same is true with you. Your job is not just to make your people laugh, smile, pumped up, and enthused. Your job is to help them to live and become like Jesus.

3. Church is where you should deal with your problems, not deny them.

Most church members think that Sunday morning is the time to focus on Jesus and that we must leave all of our worldly problems outside the doors. We are supposed to temporarily forget what happened to us this past week. We are supposed to put any and all worldly things out of our minds and memories. The church has become the place where you temporarily ignore your problems. Church is supposedly the place where you think only about Jesus and never about the world. Is this a biblical model?

We need to propose a new way to approach church. What about focusing on Jesus, who came to save us from our sins? What about our boldly coming to the throne of grace, so we can find grace in our time of need (Heb. 4:16)? He doesn't want us to ignore our hurts; He wants us to give Him those problems! Where does God say to ignore, deny, or forget about our hurts in life? We can't forget! Do we want people to try to forget being raped or molested? Why encourage denial? Is that healthy? Doesn't He accept us in our weakness and bondage? Who said we have to leave our garbage outside? Jesus wants to recycle our garbage and bring it inside to Him! He wants to take the hurts and sins of this world (and yes, even the sexual ones) and use them for His own glory to make us more like Himself. So, let's encourage people to bring *all* their hurts with them and leave them at the cross inside of church—and not outside in the parking lot.

4. Church is where you should confess your sins, not conceal them.

It's assumed on Sunday mornings or evenings that you're rather close to God because you're sitting in church close to His people. True? And if you're so close to God and His people, it's also assumed that you are much safer and less sinful than other people who are not attending church. True? Your sins are seen to be safer and smaller and more sanitized in comparison to others. People want to feel that the safest place away from the raging world is in church. (With that prevailing mind-set, who wants to be told that they might be in church sitting next to a porn producer or child molester? That can be rather unsettling!). That's how people think. And yes, it does have an element of truth and fact, but that's why it's dangerous.

Church is the very best place to conceal your sin and have people think that you're doing great and living right.

Everyone assumes you are a good Christian since you're there, and thus few rarely ask about your soul or your sins. They assume that you're saved because you're sitting next to them (or at least, they hope so). Sin is surely in the world out there but not as much in the church, and especially not in *my* church. They'd be upset to hear that another church member or attendee was actively engaged in severe sexual sin, especially there! They'll not come back. Yes, people can hide well behind a cloak of righteousness. That has always been true and always will be. Might that be true in your setting?

Some church leaders and denominational statements have also abandoned the concept of personal sin and instead replaced it with the notion that sin is found in countries, governments, political parties, and special-interest groups—but not in individuals. Their preaching reflects their theology. Other churches focus so much on evangelism that they think sin is found out there in the world but not in the church. The world needs saving but not us. And other churches view sexual sin as *the* worst of all sin; after all, that's how the pastor preaches every Sunday!

If you decide to preach about one's need to confess and renounce sexual sin, you might be viewed as being too harsh by your members. Some of your leaders or members may think you're being too strict and that certain sexual practices are not to be preached as sin. Try preaching about abortion or same-sex attraction and see. Have your resume ready.

So, how does your church deal with sin among its members or visitors? Could they handle it if you preached so well that someone started weeping out of Holy Ghost conviction, saying how terrible they feel for molesting little children in the neighborhood? Would people run for the hills, terrified that such a person is in their midst? Would your people have any tender compassion on him? Would they head for the altar to pray with him, or will they head for the door to escape? Would your membership numbers or church attendance go down? Would a real sincere sexual sinner find much mercy from your current church environment?

Would your church members show mercy to a woman who finally and humbly confesses to those sitting next to her about having an affair and abortion, after you just preached about either? How would people react if a man stands up in the midst of your wisely crafted sermon to proclaim that he does watch child porn and desperately needs help from this addiction? Does your church offer an environment in which a person feels enough security, love, and acceptance that people who are broken by your sermon will risk *all* to seek help? Do they truly feel free to confess their sins, publicly and verbally? Would they get a smug or a hug from your people? Do your people view sexual sin as the unpardonable sin—making all the sexually wounded and addicted want to hide under a rock and never come out to confess? That's the case with most churches.

Both you and your church leaders/members need to firmly believe, "Whoever conceals their sins does not prosper, but the one who confesses and renounces them finds mercy" (Prov. 28:13). Create an environment in which this happens.

5. **Preaching about sex does not mean that you are guilty of sexual sin.**

One well-known preacher from the past was caught in a national sexual scandal and said, "Pastors, I have hurt you and I have made your load heavier." How true! Today, it is so much harder to talk about sex from the pulpit because of sexual scandals involving those in religious positions. We've all been executed, already. In the church around the world, there are news headlines, allegations, and convictions of sexual misbehavior which were covered up or pushed aside. Imagine how suspicious the parish is when a priest begins to open his mouth and talks about sexual abuse of children (even though he is trying to heal, not hide). Pastors and preachers are the easiest targets on earth for sexual accusation and immediate execution. *People suspect that you are preaching about sex out of guilt for what you are hiding or doing, don't they?* They assume you're preaching to yourself in the pulpit, since their church surely doesn't have such sin in their pews. So, you do have to be careful in how often you mention this. Definitely don't mention sexual sin or sadness every single Sunday. Don't overemphasize the issue but also don't underemphasize it. Preach about sex with a truly biblical quality and quantity. Be careful not to go too far or not to go far enough—because of this prevailing perception that you're instantly guilty if you're verbal about sexual issues.

6. **The podium or pulpit is designed for communication, not adoration.**

People have idealistically romanticized the pulpit as if it were made out of the wood from the cross of Jesus, the ark of the covenant, or some other holy icon. Have you yet seen how people get so easily upset about an actual pulpit when something questionable is ever done to it or shown from it? The same applies to a metal stand or speaker's podium. Church folks have a tendency to protect and defend this area. Try to imagine the response from your church members if you were to ever show a beer bottle, pack of cigarettes, package of condoms, or adult magazine from the pulpit or podium for any reason. You might have signed your death warrant as their pastor. Many will complain to you or gossip about you as a result. The pulpit has become an object of worship in our church and is not to be tainted or tampered with. That is how some think and we can't ignore that feeling.

I once preached a sermon using a playing card with a king of hearts on it to illustrate Proverbs 22:1 about God holding the king's heart in His hands. A few commented afterward how irreverent and inappropriate it was to display a card from the pulpit. I preached another sermon using a hammer to nail into a piece of wood, trying to illustrate God's sovereignty. And yes, some people got upset and said it was wrong to do that on the pulpit. Pulpits are pure—that's how some think. Just beware of such a prevailing mind-set as it pertains to your sexual topics. Sexual language and wording from the pulpit is also seen by most people as highly irreverent and quite inappropriate. (Funny how those same church members don't get upset when sex is preached from the pulpit in their own home, called a television set—but we won't go there now.)

Try moving away from the pulpit/podium area the first few times you preach about the lessons you've learned in this book and move closer to your people in the front instead. That achieves both goals and it's a win-win situation. *Try placing some important words or phrases on the large monitor screen instead of saying them from the pulpit, if applicable. Just be careful.* You need to protect yourself from the complaints of some. By showing your words instead of saying them, you get to wisely project yourself as a warm and compassionate pastor who understands how people can be hurt. View the podium or pulpit as a yellow light to proceed with caution, instead of a red light for you to stop immediately.

7. **Good preaching can also be gentle and soft, instead of harsh and loud.**

Some church members or leaders today think that good preaching always has to be long, loud, mean, harsh, and bold. Some ministry leaders think the opposite in that all preaching should be soft, tender, emotional, and never bold or loud. Both camps are off the mark.

Good preaching is preaching that best illustrates the text or topic that has been carefully and prayerfully chosen.

If the text is about God's mercy or forgiveness, you'd better not sound harsh and mean. If your text is about God's judgment, you'd better not sound soft and gentle. Why should our voices and sermons always sound the same every single Sunday, regardless of the text? *Your tone of voice and manner of delivery should be totally dependent on your text and not on your personality.* Most preachers have never yet understood that essential deep truth.

Ministering to people with sexual wounds will require a softer and gentler tone of voice. If you've been taught by your denomination, seminary, mentor or leader not to have that kinder tone of voice in preaching, you'll never have people come to you for help and hope. You'll have already scared them far away and will continue to do so. If you yell a lot from the pulpit, people will assume that you will yell at them if they come to you for counseling. *If you are tender in your tone, they'll be more apt to believe that you will understand them in their sin or grief.* It's about time we imitate the preaching and pastoral style of Paul who said, "Our attitude among you was one of tenderness, rather like that of a devoted nurse among her babies" and that "we dealt with each one of you personally, like a father with his own children, stimulating your faith and courage and giving you instruction" (1 Thess. 2:7–12, Phillips). Good preaching, like God's voice, can sound like a gentle breeze, a soft rain, a gentle whisper or a small voice (1 Kings 19). We have to get past the false notion that our voice and style should be just like the television preachers, who typically sound far too forceful and aggressive about everything they say in their sermons! Wise preaching should change with the text or topic. God's personality is robust and diverse—so should your preaching be.

Here are some other factors or characteristics about your church that will help you decide when they might be ready to embrace such a ministry:

LOCATION: Is your church located in a densely populated area or college town? You will have greater liberty to engage in sexual topics like date rape, abortion, premarital sex, molestation, homosexuality, and pornography than if you're in a less populated and in a more rural church setting. If your church is in a small town, please be extra-careful in your sermons, because of the church gossipers who especially can ruin lives in these smaller settings. Is your church in a busier city that has a lot of runaways? Ever think that they ran away to avoid being molested by their dad or stepfather? Human trafficking is real. Regional and cultural considerations matter here too. Certain parts of the country are more inclined to accept and tolerate sexual topics or language than other areas of the country. Some will label your preaching as "gutter talk," while others will gladly say you are "telling it like it is." For example, Southerners are very different than Northerners when it comes to acceptable pulpit language about sexuality.

NUMBERS AND GENDERS: If there are only a handful of teenage girls or college-age women Sunday mornings and you continually talk about abortion, will not everyone assume one of them is probably guilty of this? If there are only a handful of men in the congregation and you rant and rave about pornography, all will suspect that one of them is the culprit and reason. If there are only a few families that have young children and you often mention child molestation in your sermons, then that family might leave, lest they be deemed the targets. If there are only a few married couples amidst the many singles attending while you mention marital sexual reluctance or refusal in your sermons, everyone assumes it's targeted.

Obviously, you are free to preach about any and all of these touchy sexual topics when you have a larger number of people—male and female, with all ages represented—who attend. Just be mindful of the intricate makeup and mind-set of your members.

AGES: People react differently to sexual topics from the pulpit depending on their age. We all know that the elderly in your church may sometimes react more negatively since they were not brought up in a culture in which sex was as freely discussed as it is today. They can be easily shocked at *any* sexual topic discussed, especially from a preacher. Age is a factor to be reckoned with.

However, do *not* assume they will all and always be repulsed. They have never told you that they have family members who have been hurt by sexual sin.

Some elderly folks have very unpleasant sexual memories of their own, as well as family secrets with their children or grandchildren that they have been hiding for a very long time now.

They didn't tell you about their sixteen-year-old granddaughter who had an abortion, that their thirty-eight-year-old daughter was recently raped, or that their twenty-seven-year-old son has same-sex attraction. Would it not be wonderful if you were the one pastor who could finally set them all free? Some older folks may welcome you with open arms because you are the first pastor to use the Bible to welcome their family's sexual suffering or secrets with open arms. And yes, they would be so proud of their preacher.

Let's go the other direction...

What do we do with the children during church?

Pulpit language about sex becomes quite tricky, as a result. Children are a force to be reckoned with when it comes to a pulpit ministry to the sexually wounded and addicted. I suggest a separate children's church service, in order to give you a little more freedom (which is all you really need) to talk more openly about this topic. All of this partially depends on whether parents are talking to their own kids about sex in their own homes. If the topic is taboo at home, don't expect anything different at church. However, some parents want you and your Sunday School teachers to approach this topic in appropriate ways in church so they can more easily discuss it at home. (You've got to admit, though, how hilarious and hypocritical it is when parents get *very* upset if their children hear about sex from the pulpit, but don't get upset when their kids hear about sex from the television set, computer screen, or school curricula. But that's another topic, isn't it?). It is interesting that the Old and New Testament scriptures were read to the entire congregation, and there is a whole lot of sexual language there that children heard.

EVENINGS AND EVENTS: How about introducing the topic of sex in a more casual and flexible setting instead, such as Sunday or Wednesday evening services? You probably have a little more freedom (again, that is all you need at first) to preach about topics usually considered taboo on Sunday mornings. Evening meetings are usually more apt to include the congregation talking with testimonies; what a neat opportunity it would be to hear how God healed others in these weaknesses, and how He set some free from their lifelong habits. Encourage members to publicly testify of such sexual miracles in their lives during evening services.

You might want to use a local or national headline event that is being discussed as a springboard or platform to approach a sexual topic in church.

Each new week there is something generated in the news which could be a starting place, true? There won't be as much protest or anger then from your members. People are talking about it; why shouldn't you? Jesus would often take a well-known event in his day as an introduction or illustration in His sermons; go and do likewise. He knew exactly what they were thinking before He spoke and while He spoke (Matt. 9:5; Luke 5:22; 6:8; 11:17). Analyze your audience and scratch them where they itch. We want them to know that God's Word talks about everything.

Now that we've examined whether your church might be ready for such a ministry, let's see if the pastor, church leaders, and staff members are equally ready for this:

1. Are your motives clean?

Do you really have a genuine compassion for sexually wounded or addicted people, or do you really want to be stimulated in a seemingly safer environment? If you're easily tempted with heterosexual or homosexual attractions, how will you help the woman or man who meets with you to discuss their sexual struggles? What will you think or do while you are alone with them? Should you simply delegate congregational counseling needs to specialized staff who have also read this book? Does your budget allow this? Do you need to have someone else there at this time? Is this asking for too much temptation? It might be. Do you want to know people's sexual histories in order to help them or so you can be turned on as you ponder these scenarios later on? If you're not having a healthy and happy amount of sexual activity in your marriage, please deal with that first. Do you ask for more details to learn more, or to lust more? That's important. Your goal is to find the facts and not feed your fantasies.

Don't assume your motives are as clean as you think. "The heart is deceitful above all things and beyond cure. Who can understand it?" (Jer. 17:9).

You need squeaky-clean motives for being pastorally involved with those who have become sexually involved.

Whoever wants to stand in His holy place must have clean hands and a pure heart (Ps. 24:3–4). How strong are you if the vulnerable woman you're counseling feels the need to prove her desirability and femininity and you happen to become her safer target? You will not believe the immense quantity and quality of sexual temptations that will come your way should you become well known as a skilled and compassionate counselor and preacher who really does understand sexually hurting and broken people. Make yourself *very* accountable to others in practical ways as you enter this monstrous minefield.

Your sex life needs to be happy, as it is. Your marriage needs to be happy, as it is. If there are problems in either, you're not ready to minister.

2. Is your past forgiven?

You can't minister from personal lust and you can't minister out of past guilt.

If you have unresolved guilt from past sexual misbehavior, you're not yet ready. Are you truly preaching to others, *or*, might you be vicariously preaching to or about yourself? If you're tormented about sex, it will show up sooner or later. Preaching about sex does not make God forgive you of any or all your past sexual indiscretions. Only the blood of Jesus cleanses you from all sin (1 John 1:7) and that includes sexual sin. You have to personally experience this grace to preach it. If you have sexual issues from your past that are not resolved (and you might), how can you show others how their similar issues can be resolved? Have a long talk with God before you tell others to do the same. He who is forgiven much, loves much (Luke 7:47). They will see your freedom and be attracted to it.

3. Is your job secure?

If your leadership is not currently supportive of you right now, you might need to wait to preach on sex or you might end up waiting in the unemployment line. You might need monies set aside, just in case they choose to set *you* aside. If they don't love your current preaching, this will be the straw that breaks the camel's back. Having your people supportive of you is quite instrumental and foundational. If they have been looking for *any* reason to dismiss you, this will certainly become the one reason they will easily and quickly use. Timing is everything.

If you are brand new and they expect you to keep the peace and not make any waves, wait. Gain their trust or respect first.

People need to trust you before they allow you to enter their holy of holies.

Few people, if any, will ever be allowed to enter their sacred room of sexual wounds, sins, temptations, and memories. Will you be one of those few who are given access to their sexual secrets and sadness? I hope so. What better person than their pastor who will most fervently pray for them and shepherd them!

This next chapter helps you to see that you're in good company and following in the footsteps of a good God who has given you the green light to enter within. He never was embarrassed to talk about sexual topics since the beginning of time.

3

THE BIRDS AND THE BEES AND THE BIBLE

Today's sexual activities are the same as in the Old and New Testaments. Indeed, there is nothing new under the sun (Eccl. 1:9). Believe it or not, we did not invent sexual promiscuity, frequency, curiosity, or activity. Christians in the early New Testament church lived in a society much like ours, saturated with sexuality. Men participated naked in the Olympic Games. Corinth had a temple at Aphrodite with more than ten thousand cult prostitutes. The Greeks had a proverb that "women are for breeding but boys are for pleasure." Seneca said that any married woman who confined herself to two illicit affairs was a rare and virtuous creature. Pornographic sexual positions practiced in Pompeii were revealed beneath the volcanic ash of Mount Vesuvius. Sappho, with her school for girls in the

Isle of Lesbos (yes, from which we get "lesbian"), had a love affair with another woman who did not return her affection, so she drowned herself. Sound familiar today? The Apostle Paul said that we'd have to literally leave the world in order to escape from people who are involved in sexual sin (1 Cor. 5:10). Sexual sin (and the emotional effects of these sins) is no surprise to biblical writers. Jesus was neither shocked, intimidated, nor repulsed by those who were sexually active. He did not think it was inappropriate or beneath Him to be with "sexual sinners." He freely socialized with, and ministered to, the most sexually active people of His time. Unfortunately, His ministry to the sexually wounded and addicted was a sore spot and stumbling block to the religious leaders of His time.

He never once fell into temptation; instead, He helped people to fall in love with His Heavenly Father. Yes, you can do the same. You can stay pure even while ministering to people who are perceived as impure. Your church should daily minister to people whom the religious people will daily avoid. Will you do the same and be like Jesus? Jesus was constantly being criticized for hanging around those who had truly been around. In John 4, we see Him witnessing to the woman at the well who had been married five times and was living with another man at the time. Jesus was not at all embarrassed to bring up her sex life and freely discuss it with her. In Luke 7, He allows a woman with a bad reputation to engage Him in tender repentance. In Luke 15, He is criticized for allowing sexual and other sinners to approach Him. Jesus was never afraid of what others would think of His ministry. We will always have to face this fear of what others might think of our counseling clientele, church attenders, community seekers, and casual company.

God knew that new converts to His family needed help with this topic of sex. Sexual thoughts and behaviors were some of His first priorities. (See Acts 15:28–31; 21:25; Gal. 5:19–21; Eph. 4:17–24; 5:2; and Col. 3:5–8.) He talks of controlling sexual desires in 1 Thessalonians 4:3–7. He speaks about incest, intercourse, immorality, adultery, male and female prostitutes, virginity, burning, and homosexuality to the Corinthian church. He was not afraid to preach or talk about sex, like so many are today. He covers it all.

Other New Testament writers bring up sex in their sermons, just as explicitly. Peter spoke about people whose goals in life were committing adultery and seducing others in 2 Peter 2:14–19. Hebrews 13:4 discusses sex in marriage being kept pure. Jude was aware that lustful and immoral people secretly slipped into the congregation. God warned His people about a woman who tempted others into sexual immorality in Revelation 2:20–25. These revolutionary New Testament epistles were publicly read to the whole congregation. There were no Internet websites or blogs, Facebook posts, voice mails or emails, scanned documents, or laser printers. *Whatever was written—was read —out loud—to the whole congregation—including children.*

In Deuteronomy 4, Moses also tells parents to teach their children *all* the lessons that happened and many of these are sexual and found even in Genesis.

In Genesis 1, there's a man and wife totally naked yet unashamed of their bodies. Genesis 12 describes Pharaoh's sexual attraction to Sarai. Chapter 19 openly talks of an attempted homosexual gang rape, as well as incestuous relations between a father and daughters. Genesis 26:8 is quite beautiful where God describes Isaac caressing his wife Rebekah. God later describes a horrible rape scene in chapter 34 and talks of incest in chapter 35.

Genesis 38 has another story you hear little about. When is the last time you heard a sermon about a man who spills his seed in sexual intercourse? Ever heard a sermon about a man's one-night stand that happened to be with his daughter-in-law? Genesis 38 is not the most sought-out sermon material today for preachers.

Yet, Genesis 39 is probably the most famous chapter that is sermon material. Joseph answers sexual temptation by simply saying he won't sin against his God.

Why do we *only* hear sermons about sex from Genesis 39 and not from all the other chapters in Genesis that equally and carefully describe a much wider range of behavior? Why is there such silence and selectivity in our sermons about sex from Genesis?

The Bible is consistent in listing sexual sin *not* at the top of lists, but rather in the midst of "sin lists." Sexual—and nonsexual—sins are listed side by side and all together (Deut. 27; Rom. 1:18–32; 1 Cor. 6:9–11; Gal. 5:16–21; Eph. 5:3–7; Col. 3:5–10; 1 Tim. 1:8–11; 1 Peter 4:2–5; Jude 4–16). *Sexual sin happens to be listed as one sin among many sins, and not as the one sin above all other sins.* It is *not* the unpardonable sin, is it? Then, why do we speak of it as such?

Did you know that David's murder of Uriah is mentioned more often than his affair with Bathsheba, as God records David's different sins of his past? David is called "a man of bloods" and not "a man of lust" as *the* reason for his being barred from building the temple (2 Sam. 12; 16:5–8). God was not pleased with what he did to Bathsheba but He was even more displeased with what he did to Uriah. Why do we preach about David's sexual sin to the exclusion of the others?

Did you know that Sodom and Gomorrah was guilty of much more than homosexuality as the reason for their downfall? God said they were arrogant, overfed, and unconcerned about helping the poor and needy in Ezekiel 16:49–50. Why do we tend to selectively and conveniently ignore these other nonsexual and social justice sins when we only emphasize their homosexual sin? Have you done this?

Fornication and covetousness are also mentioned side by side in the New Testament list of vices to avoid (1 Cor. 10:7–14; Rev. 22:15). Both are listed as idolatry. Sex, like money, can easily become one's god. Jesus spoke more about money than sex. Why are we so vocal about sex, yet so very silent about greed?

Yes, God wants His people to be sexually different from the prevailing culture. He always has and always will. In contrast to the full nudity of the sacred sexual Canaanite cults and drunken sex orgies of the Egyptians, Babylonians, and Assyrians, God commanded His people to wear long robes, wash their clothes, and refrain from sex (Ex. 19:14–15; 20:26; 28:42–43) so they could be better prepared for worship. God made us male and female and He knows the mysteriously woven connection that exists between the physical, emotional, and spiritual parts of our being. That's why He protects it before and restricts it within marriage. Pastors need to talk a lot more about God encouraging this spousal sexual activity to be frequently and joyfully experienced in 1 Corinthians 7:1–5.

Except for necrophilia and masturbation, God addresses pretty much any and every sexual behavior in the Bible from the very first chapter (Gen. 1:27) to the very last chapter (Rev.

22:15). The frequency and frankness will amaze and surprise you as you begin to research and review this.

Here are some examples:

Leviticus 18 and 20 openly discusses sexual intercourse with other family members, neighbors, and even animals. God was not afraid to speak of people having sex with animals (Exod. 22:16-19; Deut. 27:21). He also talks about men wearing women's clothes, sexually seducing someone, testing for virginity, adultery, rape, and incest in Deuteronomy 22. Judges 19 describe a gang rape and sexual abuse. Amos 2:7 speaks of a father and son sexually using the same woman, while 1 Samuel 18:24–27 mentions one hundred foreskins with simplicity and no apology. Deuteronomy 25:11–12 speaks of a man's privates, Deuteronomy 23:9–14 openly talks about nocturnal emissions and physical excrements and 1 Samuel 24:3 describes a man relieving himself. Bathroom and bedroom behavior are both included in God's holy words.

Ezekiel 23 shows us that God is not prudish in discussing sex. Here, He speaks of genitals like those of donkeys, seminal emissions like those of horses, lusting for and fondling young virgin breasts, and nakedness. He then talks about using a woman for all that she is. Yes, the chapter is mostly meant to symbolize the unfaithfulness of Israel but it is noteworthy that God used intensely graphic sexual language without any apology whatsoever. First Corinthians 7:1–7 deals openly with marital sexual intercourse, while Proverbs 5:19–20 commands the husband to embrace and be captivated with the breasts of his wife. Proverbs 6 and 7 describe a sexual seduction and adulterous affair, with the surprise consequences discussed later. Second Samuel 13:1–21 is a true account of a deceptive and dysfunctional family sexual assault and abuse scene that rarely is ever preached. Did you happen to preach on any of these biblical stories, characters, texts, or lessons recently?

The Song of Solomon is one of God's most descriptive stories about sex, where He employs a variety of sexual situations and picturesque words to make His point. How unfortunate and unbelievable that this book has been allegorized, symbolized, and spiritualized to mean something that God never intended. We laugh at Origen allegorizing the Good Samaritan story, but

most preachers do the same thing here. Yes, it can symbolize
the marriage relationship the believer has with Christ and their
keeping themselves faithful to each other and pure as a symbol
of what God desires in our relationship with Him and with our
spouse (Isa. 54:5; 61:10–11; 62:5; Jer. 2:2; Hos. 2:14–23; Rom.
9:25; 2 Cor. 11:2–3; Eph. 3:11–13; 5:22–31), but you can not
avoid or escape the obvious references to sexuality. This is one
great book—but it is not an easy book to understand with the
shifting of speakers, lack of chronology, abundance of symbols,
and some sudden interruptions by a chorus to make transitions
from one scene to another. A Victorian mind-set of modesty,
combined with a religious taboo on this topic, has clouded and
muffled a careful exegesis and exposition of Song of Solomon.
When you look into the original Hebrew language that God
uses and then compare it with how those words are used in the
cultural background, you'll be truly amazed at how romanti-
cally, openly, accurately, and beautifully God speaks about our
sexuality in marriage.

Our male and female genitalia are individually described—
metaphorically and euphemistically. *In Proverbs 5, our sexual
organs are described as plants, vines, stalks, fruits, gardens,
doors, streams, wells, walls, and fountains.* You have to remember that fact because it provides the foundation for the
Song of Solomon. God describes their sexual married interac-
tion with visually erotic words—not mere boring physiological
or medical ones. This book describes sexual marital love in
erotic and poetic words that are light years ahead of our time.
Solomon and Shulamite surely weren't bashful or boring in the
bedroom, not even close.

They took their sex quite seriously—not as something to
be toyed with or taken lightly. You don't see them engaging in
the pettiness and tease of premarital fondling; they are satisfied
with nothing less than the sheer ecstasy of orgasm and release
through full sexual intercourse and consummation. God wants
the husband and wife to be fully sexually aroused by each other
(Song 2:7; 3:5; 8:4) and to save that sacred act of intercourse
for each other. The Shulamite couldn't wait to totally and sexually give herself to her husband (4:12–16; 5:1) and they both
describe and delight in entering, enjoying, and even tasting the
bodily parts of their loved one. They compliment each other
on their sexual skills. Her sexual aggressiveness, ability, and

enjoyment is evident. She verbally encourages and actively participates in their lovemaking. She yearns for him to fondle her breasts while he is completely overwhelmed by their beauty. She invites him and asks him to enter into her moistened and scented garden of delights (4:10–5:1). Ever heard a sermon like this from Song of Solomon 4–8?

It's about time for preachers to publicly be thankful to God for sexuality. Sex should be taken seriously but thankfully. It is a gift God gave to us, just like other gifts. He created us male and female, and it was *good.* Satan tries to mess up this wonderful gift, and he has done quite a marvelous job doing just that. Christians need to remember that the human body and sexual intercourse were beautifully designed by God Himself. It is *not* dirty or evil because it is physical and sensual—let's abandon this gnostic notion of our bodies.

The only thing we hear today from the church is totally negative about sexual expression before marriage and it's about time we hear some positive sermons about sexual expression within marriage.

God was not eager to address any sexual topics but neither was He reluctant. That should be our pattern. His sexual language is not prudish, but neither is it prurient. He is not shy or embarrassed, even if we are. God didn't give us a red light or a stop sign—instead, He gave us a yellow light to proceed with caution as we approach this difficult and delicate topic. The Bible gives us the big picture of the reasons, and also the remedies, for sexual sin or sadness. God shows us the causes and the consequences, along with the consolation He offers to those who need deeper emotional healing. He expects us to know this and show this to a hurting world. Based on the content we've learned in this chapter, let's see how we can best demonstrate, imitate, and communicate this good news in the next chapter.

PREPARING YOUR MESSAGE

4

HOW YOU CAN PREACH ABOUT SEX, YET STILL KEEP YOUR JOB

A travel agency sued the Yellow Pages for advertising in their phone book that their agency specialized in "erotic" tours—when it was supposed to say "exotic." Oops! Just a difference of one small letter resulted in a huge flood of interested (but disappointed) callers, as well as a lawsuit. Mark Twain said "the difference between the right word and the almost right word is the difference between lightning and a lightning bug."

Death or life resides in the power of the tongue (Prov. 18:21), and the purpose of this chapter is to help you choose words that bring life and not death. This is the hardest part.

Choosing the right words is the most delicate but difficult task for preachers who want to minister to sexually wounded and addicted people.

We can and must use the same type of words that God uses in the Scriptures when it comes to sexual language from the pulpit. *Here are ten uniquely different principles or biblical patterns you should learn:*

1. Plan ahead and write out your pulpit sexual language.

When it comes to sex, don't try to preach spontaneously or off the cuff. Resist the temptation to just wing it here, as you might do with the rest of your sermon. Go through the painstakingly slow but important process of writing down your words about sex, so that you can hear them before others will hear them. Memorize your vitally important section where you employ emotional and sexual language in whatever way it takes for you to smoothly deliver. Use whatever mnemonic or electronic device you need to say it right—podium or teleprompter. That is exactly what I have done for you in the last half of this book with our difficult taboo topics. Review and rehearse your words over and over again so that it sounds right. How would sexually wounded or addicted people hear your words? This is just far too important.

When you are starting out, you must write it down. Do not trust your brain to instinctively or casually say the right words as you construct your sermon with sexual wording. *You don't have to say a lot, but you do have to plan a lot.* Seamless transitions and wise segues are not easy to construct in your message! It is very hard work for those who want to hone their craft and upgrade their preaching skills.

2. Your ultimate goal here is ministry, not controversy.

Preaching about sex is all about individuals, not about issues. You're not delivering a manuscript—you're delivering people out of bondage. Your goal is never to draw attention to your sermon's sexual content but to draw people to Jesus. Don't give people any more rationale or reasons to criticize you here. Your words are a mean to an end, not an end in itself. You want to minister to people's hearts and not scratch their itching ears. You'll literally see people sit up, lift their heads up, and have their eyes tear up when you speak about sexual hurt—but don't be fooled by this newfound attention. When you get their attention, lift up the Lord Jesus. Encourage them to lay down their worries and wounds at the cross of Jesus As you speak difficult words with delicate connotations, your goal is to stir up the Spirit of God and not stir up controversy. If that is where your heart is, your words will follow (Matt. 12:34). You get to see the Spirit of God breaking through.

You don't need to draw attention to sexual language by ever apologizing for it. God does not apologize in the Scriptures for doing it. Why should you? *Don't draw attention to what you say but instead, emphasize why you say these words.* Talk to your people like a tender shepherd addressing his or her wayward lost sheep. People won't be as inclined to criticize your message when they see your motives.

3. Use a modern translation of the Bible.

Do not use an outdated and antiquated translation of the Bible with lots of watered-down or strange words you'll have to explain later in your sermon. Compare Genesis 26:8 in the King James Version ("Isaac was sporting with Rebekah, his wife") to the same Genesis 26:8 in other versions, which describe Isaac as caressing, hugging, kissing, fondling, or making love to his wife. Intimacy is intended in the Hebrew word used by God. Why take the time to try and explain what in the world "sporting" means in our language, when you don't have to? You truly open yourself to saying something less than perfect when you say more words on sex. Compare the KJV of Deuteronomy 25:11, describing a woman "who putteth forth her hand, and taketh him by the secrets" to the much better translations where "she reaches out and seizes him by his private parts [or sex organs, or genitals]." Compare the different wordings of all the translations for Genesis 39:7 about what Potiphar's wife said to Joseph. There are so many other examples that could be given and I hope you see my point here. It's actually fascinating research to do.

Why should you become an easy and instant target when you don't have to? Let the accurate modern translations do the delicate and dirty work instead of you trying to explain. Why use an old-fashioned translation when you don't have to? I know that some of you will only use certain translations whenever you preach. Why try to explain these sexual details and open yourself to more criticism? This will make your job a lot easier. Use the exact same words that God used, in an understandable translation, so that you won't be accused of using any suggestive or soiled language from the pulpit.

4. Brevity and quality is much better than quantity.

Sex is so explosive that just a small spark will ignite and cause a combustion. A slight touch of a fresh wound is all that it takes to get someone's attention. Be wise, not wordy, when it comes to your sexual language from the pulpit. The more you say, the bigger of a hole you're going to dig for yourself.

> *You don't need to preach a whole sermon about any sexual topic—all you need to do is to carefully construct key sections with wisely chosen words and sentences in your sermons.*

People *will* certainly remember those few and rare phrases or sentences that mentioned sex. You just said something that they've probably never heard from the pulpit. You should plan and know exactly which words, phrases, or sentences you will use. You should know when, where, and why. Sometimes use a pause to reinforce your point and let it sink in—and then go on. But don't pause too long after you use sexual words, since people will then get uneasy. *There is an art to when you pause and how long you pause in preaching, especially when it comes to emotional or sexual language.*

Another reason to say little is because God does. You don't have to go into a lot of sexual detail because God doesn't. Even the most famous sex scenes in the Bible have little detail upon a closer examination of the text. Second Samuel 11:4 describes David and Bathsheba: "She came to him, and he slept with her." Second Samuel 13:14 describes Amnon's rape of Tamar as "he raped her." Judges 19:25 says "they raped her and abused her throughout the night." God could have described the many details and nuances in each of these sexual scenes, but He did not. God could have said *so* much more about these sexual scenes, but He didn't.

God purposefully omitted the steamy sexual details as He directed the writers of Scripture as to exactly what to include or not include (2 Peter 1:20–21). This same biblical pattern is true when describing Samson and Delilah. God says very little about the incest and homosexuality in the church at Corinth. He doesn't describe the type of sexual immorality that went on in the church over at Thyatira. The list could go on. Just imagine what today's television or movie producer would do with these Bible stories in terms of describing these sexual bedroom scenes and what they were or were not wearing, the orgasms they experienced, and the performances they gave. God didn't do that, did He? His ways are so far above and beyond our ways. So why do you think He does this? Here's the answer:

5. **Your ultimate goal is to teach, not tempt, as you preach about sex.**

As you study the Bible, you'll be fascinated to learn that God does not dwell on what happens before or during the sexual scenes of Scripture but instead, He *does* dwell on what happens afterward as a result of the sexual behavior He described! He wants us to learn, not lust. Education—not imagination, stimulation, or titillation—is His goal, and that must be yours also. Never forget this point.

The cities of Sodom and Gomorrah were removed by God. The incest of Lot with his daughters produced two nations of wicked people who troubled Israel. Revenge on Shechem's rape of Dinah resulted in the murder of every man in the city. The sexual sin of Reuben in Genesis 35:22 is exposed and punished later in 49:3–4. The lust of Potiphar's wife sent an innocent man to prison. The lust of Samson brought both his and his nation's downfall. David's adultery led to the death of an innocent man and also of his infant son. Amnon's rape of Tamar prompted Absalom's murder of Amnon. Solomon's sexual partners caused him to stray from God and bring judgment on the nation.

See the biblical pattern here?

When God describes these sexual situations in the Scriptures, He is much more interested in stimulating our holiness rather than our hormones in everyday life. Your preaching about sex must reflect the same priorities that God has for us. Your goal is to appeal to our higher and not our lower natures.

After describing (briefly, of course) the sexual immorality in 1 Corinthians 10 which was taken from Exodus 32, we're told His reason in verses 11 to 13: God wants us to learn from this! God also did not go into great detail about David's sin with Bathsheba in Psalms 32 and 51. He didn't describe Rahab's past promiscuous lifestyle, but He did describe her obedience afterward in Joshua 2. The same is true of the woman in John 4; we're told of her testimony to others as a result. We're not given the details about the ex-homosexuals in 1 Corinthians 6, but only the fact that they were indeed changed by God's power. We're also not told about the details of the sexual misbehavior in 2 Corinthians 2, but only about the proper treatment of this man who was guilty of this. *Even some of the Bible's most unbelievably sexually graphic chapters (Ezekiel 16 and 23) are there to teach us some deeply spiritual lessons in life (16:30–63; 23:28–49).* Again, the physical and sexual language in Deuteronomy 23:9–13 ends with a spiritual lesson in verse 14 to be holy.

6. Convey hope and healing, not just hatred, in sermons.

It's so important to offer a critically necessary and desperately needed biblical balance in the same message when it comes to talking about sex in your sermons. Few ever do. Most sermons on abortion leave the impression that God is disgusted with the woman who did it. Rarely is there any mention of God's forgiveness or hope offered to the woman who chose this, to the parents or boyfriend who insisted upon this, or to the doctor who performed this.

This includes all sexual topics in our sermons. I've heard my fair share of "gay-bashing" or "gay acceptance" sermons, but not "gay healing" sermons. Why are we so one-sided? Sermons full of references to casual sex, same-sex attraction, or pornography rarely offer people a second chance and new beginnings—but God does. Always include the future with the past. "What did you do in the past?" could be improved by adding the new thought of "What will you do in the future?" If your goal is to make people feel guilty—or feel good—as a result of your sermons, you're not including both truth *and* grace. Again, let's look at biblical precedence and pattern.

Jesus doesn't publicly condemn the woman's sexual sin but He also shares the good news of the gospel with the sexually active woman in John 4 and then with the sexually active woman in Luke 7:36–50. He offers them hope. Paul tells the Corinthian church to forgive the repentant man who was guilty of incest in 2 Corinthians 2:5–11. Paul also offers God's transforming grace for all the many different church members who used to be sexually selfish in 1 Corinthians 6:9–18.

Let's promise God that we'll never again speak publicly or privately against any sexual practice or activity *without equally sharing* the glorious hope, grace, mercy, pardon, and victory available for those who are in Christ Jesus.

7. Use sexual euphemisms and alternative language here.

When you preach about sex, you must be so very careful with the words that you choose. Without realizing it, you can severely hurt people's fragile feelings and communicate something that you really didn't want to intend to verbalize.

I remember a sermon where the pastor was describing a woman who had a wild past before she was a Christian. She fell in love with a godly man, and the pastor was giving them premarital counseling sessions. He wanted each to know the other's sexual history and used these specific words in his sermon: "I wanted this man to realize that he was getting a used car and not the new car he thought he had ordered." This pastor meant well but it didn't come across well. Ouch! Should everyone who has had premarital sex now view themselves as a used car? What about the woman who was raped, or the child who was molested? How would they feel now? Are they used cars now, too? Is that the best choice of words? Let's do better!

Review the Song of Solomon again, and observe His wise usage of words. God tells us that "Adam knew Eve," instead of saying he had full sexual intercourse with her. We sometimes read that people "fell asleep," instead of the fact they had died. God sometimes uses euphemisms to gently soften a harsher wording. Do the same.

Here are some suggestions for alternate sexual language from the pulpit:

- *A woman's breasts?* Her bosom or chest.
- *Penis or vagina?* Their reproductive organs.
- *Condoms?* Male contraceptives.
- *Sexual Intercourse?* They became intimate with each other; they had relations together; they did what husbands and wives are allowed and supposed to do.
- *Sexual Refusal / Reluctance / Resistance / Rejection?* Hesitant to offer one's body to his or her spouse; doesn't yet freely and fully give himself or herself to one's spouse; timid to be intimate; not interested in physical or sexual expression.
- *Fornication?* They were sexually active; they lost their virginity; they gave into temptation; they compromised their standards; they didn't wait for marriage; they became physically involved before they should have.
- *Pornography?* Sexually explicit materials or visuals; adult viewing; erotic images of others besides your spouse.
- *Rape?* He sexually assaulted her; he took advantage of her; he forced himself upon her; he violated her; he overpowered her.
- *Masturbation?* Solo sex.
- *Homosexual?* A same-sex attraction; a gender-identity crisis.
- *Childhood Sexual Abuse or Molestation?* He tricked her into doing things that only husbands and wives do; he treated her like a wife instead of a daughter.

   Interchange these many different sexual words at different times in a sermon. If I can, I use the biblical euphemism or the softer sexual wording, but usually I'll end with the most commonly used words that they understand and use daily. It's good to ultimately end with the strongest word. She is not telling herself that she was taken advantage of—she knows she was *raped!* A violent act needs an equally violent word sometimes, to get their attention and emotions.

8. Use emotional words to draw out sexual memories.

People have *very* good memories whenever their sexuality is violated. Chemically and emotionally, these memories are implanted in their minds. Sometimes the sexual pain is so excruciatingly intense that they will unknowingly try to erase or forget it, or even create multiple personalities or alternate worlds to live in. All you need to do is to gently touch or scratch the wound—and they feel it *now*!

Always target the emotional effects and not the sexual activity that took place. In addition to using Bible commentaries, it's helpful to also use a concordance or language lexicon to discover how that particular Hebrew or Greek word depicting the emotion or action is used elsewhere in the Scriptures. Do the homework; it's well worth it.

One particular story that has molded my ministry is how God described the feelings of Tamar after being sexually tricked and violated by Amnon in 2 Samuel 13:1–22, who was disgraced and who kept crying out loud as she left, and then lived out the rest of her life as a desolate and devastated woman. You also read about David being furious and Absalom hating Amnon, as a result. It's that total devastation, desolation, and disgrace that God will heal; it's the bondage of anger and hatred in your heart that He can dissolve. You hover over their hurt. You want to feel their pain, and feel how they felt. Take your time in imagining or visualizing the story. Research the etymology and recreate the scene of the crime in your mind. Read again that passage or story of their sexual sadness or violence.

Here are some emotional phrases I've used in drawing out sexual pain:

- No matter what someone did to you, or what you've done to them.
- No matter what difficult, painful, physical, or sexual experience you've had.
- No matter what sexual tragedy or emotional trauma you went through.
- No matter what you've done, what habits you have, who your master is.

- No matter how helpless you feel in controlling your emotions of….
- No matter what injustice you've suffered that you did not deserve.
- No matter how dark, deep, dirty, or guilty you now feel because of what you did to someone, *or* because of what someone has wrongly done to you.

Jesus understands your feelings of loss, shame, filth, anger, pain, hurt, damage, disgust, confusion, and humiliation. He gives you the strength you need to have the victory you want, when you feel so very helpless.

Use sensory rather than sensual language. The Holy Spirit knows their secret sexual wound or sin. Trust Him to remind them at the right time. As you employ emotional rather than sexual wording, you'll see the effects unfold before you.

9.   Make it known that you're compassionate and competent.

The average person identified with Jesus. They followed and liked Him. The common people flocked to Jesus. He was down to earth and people felt comfortable with Him. He did not intimidate people with the bigger words or stern face, like the religious leaders did. They really felt that He could help them. He didn't act silly or superior toward them, like the religious leaders did. Do you have that pulpit and personal presence yet? Do you convey warmth, insight, wisdom, depth, understanding, mercy, tenderness, and gentleness? Would people want to come to you for a private conversation after your sermon? Do they come to you now?

Here is a personal checklist to consider:

Your voice? Listen to yourself on tape. Listen to *how you talk* and ignore the content for now. Does it sound too tender or too tough? Do you have to speak so loudly while preaching? Or are you so mild and soft-spoken that your people don't hear authority? When you speak of sexual matters in your sermons, pause; speak slower, softly, firmly, authoritatively, and gently. *Purposefully change your tone apart from the rest of the sermon and go at a slower speed and noticeably different pace.* Do *not* keep the same predictable and regular tone when talking about sex.

Your smile? Do you have one while preaching? If not, get one soon.

Eye contact? Force yourself to look into people's eyes when you're speaking on a more emotional or sexual topic. This is not a term paper here. Do you need to change those old-fashioned eyeglasses, which make it hard for people to look into your eyes? Consider contact lenses or laser eye surgery? Eyes are crucial, especially when you're talking, preaching, or counseling about their sexual hurts.

Gestures and posture? Lean forward toward your people. Don't be so uptight and wooden. Are you invitational and approachable? Extend your arms and reach out with open hands. Again, take on a softer tone when talking of sexual pain and take on a somewhat harsher tone when talking of sexual sin. But keep in mind that you want people to feel that they can come to you as a safe haven, and not be your punching bag.

Leave the pulpit area? Buy or get that lapel microphone and use it. Sound and look invitational and approachable. Don't hide behind anything. Be their Jesus. Come out into the congregation and walk closer or amidst your people, like He did.

10. Be equally skilled at bringing comfort and conviction.

You must be skilled at bringing about totally opposite results and not just one. For some preachers, it's your style to bring comfort; for others, it's so easy to bring conviction. Which is your personality most drawn to doing? You *do* have a preference. Your training or denomination sometimes tends to dictate your preaching style; you do what you think you're expected to do and preach how others preach, right? Your spiritual gift also has a dramatic effect on how you preach or counsel. If your spiritual gift is more prophetic, you need to practice sounding nicer and more tender. If your spiritual gift is mercy, you need to practice sounding more prophetic and firmer. Which is your strength? Your strength is always your weakness, and it will work for or against you! Very few preachers are able to shift personalities and preach both styles just as easily. Some texts demand both types of preaching. Are you equally skilled at both? Can you convey both in the same sermon? Change your style, based on the text. George Whitefield said, "Every minister must be a Boanerges, a son of thunder—as well as a Barnabas, a son of consolation."

One of our jobs is to help people get past the concealing stage and move them to the confessing stage of their pain or sin. David shares how good it felt to finally confess his sexual sin and pain (Ps. 32; 51) after Nathan confronted him in 2 Samuel 12. People *need* to confess to God their sin and their pain (James 5:16).

Who is more equipped than you to help them do exactly this? That's our job. Encourage them to confess, grieve, vent, cry, verbalize what they have now internalized, remember what they repressed, or be angry at themselves or others. You never know what emotions are going to come out as both God's truth and grace begin to shine in. God is able to handle their emotions, heal their hearts, and change their habits. He's able to take our punches and change our thoughts.

The next seven chapters will examine each of the most delicate and difficult topics—the deepest and darkest sexual hurts and habits—sins and pains, addictions and agonies—as we apply the Scriptures to people in our preaching, discipleship, evangelism, and counseling. Near the end of each of the next seven chapters, there are carefully constructed and creatively crafted sermon samples, suggestions, ideas, examples, transitional segues, sentences, and sections to help you get started. These can be used in your public proclamation, professional counseling, and private conversations that you will soon have with your congregation, community, friends, and family. You will be completely ready.

5

CASUAL SEX

Rarely will you find someone who has only had one life-time sexual partner. Sexual activity no longer begins today when people get married; it usually starts in the teenage years. It's much harder and longer to wait until marriage today. Societal and peer pressure has never, ever been stronger in encouraging people to have premarital or extramarital sex. A teenager today is exposed to more sexual temptation on a school day than his grandfather ever was, even when he was out on the weekend looking for it. Premarital sexual activity is widely accepted and practiced today, both in and out of the church. No matter what numbers you quote, America still has the highest teenage pregnancy and teenage abortion rate in the world. *Our specialty must be communication to a generation deeply into fornication.* And spiritual religiosity has little effect on curbing sexual curiosity in America today, let's face it. Most younger and older adults in the church have the exact same prayer as St. Augustine: "Lord, give me chastity, but not yet."

"Getting married" has been replaced with "getting protection." Condoms have become our national savior; what would we do without them? "How you have sex" has become more important than "when you have sex." "What you have sex with" has become more important than "who you have sex with." Our message of "save sex" has been replaced by "safe sex." One little letter makes all the difference in the world! While the world is mostly concerned with result of pregnancy, the church should be mostly concerned with the root of promiscuity. Forget about parents telling their kids about sex; they just don't do it. They say they do but they don't. Go ask their teens. Teens aren't honest about what they tell their parents about sex and the parents aren't honest about talking to their teen about sex. Leaving sex education up to parents is idealistic and the church should be helping here. I haven't yet figured out why parents want their kids to learn about sex from public school teachers but not from their Sunday School teachers.

If the school mentions the topic of sex, there is relief. If the church mentions sex, there is rebellion. Why this craziness?

REASONS: We know why. This is not rocket science here. It really isn't complicated, is it? Scripture frequently acknowledges the power and presence of sexual temptation, especially in males. The book of Proverbs was written primarily to young people—especially males—and emphasizes temptation. See that sexual temptation knocking on Joseph's door in Genesis 39. We're told to "flee the evil desires of youth" in 2 Timothy 2:22. Before we begin our preaching against sex, we'd better remember *our* own youth and *our* own desires, in which we wanted to fit in with the crowd around us. There is general peer pressure and then, sometimes, it's specific personal pressure from the boyfriend or girlfriend who is requesting, allowing, seducing, or tempting them. Remember that?

Curiosity is another reason. What does it feel like? No one wants to be left out of the conversation or the crowd. Some have sex just to be able to say they did it.

Many people (regardless of age) use sex as a drug, a pain-killer, or as a physical high. It can help you temporarily forget your problems or responsibilities and we like that. God purposefully chose to make this act of sexual intercourse very pleasurable! Who doesn't like pleasure? We get stimulation, release, thrills, and sensations that are beyond the daily drudge. For many people, sex has become the drug to deliver them from emotional emptiness. It's the only thrill and sure thing in a world of depressing news and increasing stress.

Rebellion is another reason. Some engage in sex in their parents' bedroom to get even for all the hurt they feel. Children who are provoked to anger (Eph. 6:1–4) get back at their parents in a way that will hurt them even more, when discovered. Some aren't even aware of this deep-seated anger that boils over.

Independence and power are two other reasons. Casual premarital sexual activity is one of the most secretive acts that kids can do when parents are not watching or controlling them. It gives them a sense of power over their parents and makes them feel like adults for the only time in their average daily routine.

Most importantly, people use sex as a way of feeling loved in a very unloving world. They feel they don't get it from Dad or Mom so they go elsewhere. Adults should surely understand that, as they also feel unloved from their spouses and go elsewhere. Those dealing with their own demons of deprival understand the most. Mom or Dad are too busy and never home. The husband or wife is always working late and never home. Parents or spouses are on social media sites and too busy. Hungry people go anywhere to find food. Desperate people do desperate things. Instead of sitting down to talk about things with the right person, people end up laying down in bed with the wrong person.

Younger (and older) people have sex in order to finally please someone in their lives. People have parents (or spouses) who are always criticizing, demoralizing, and demeaning you. They're often told they're doing something wrong, never trying hard enough, never are good enough, or don't do what others do. Finally, we find someone who doesn't nag us but enjoys us for who we are and not what we do. Sex is a way of getting some serious revenge—from kids and/or spouses.

Finally, many people engage in premarital (or extramarital) sex simply because they already gave in before and didn't experience any consequences, as warned. We all know of the tendency to give up once we've given in. They didn't feel guilty, get caught, get pregnant, get killed by lightning, or get AIDS. Instead of all those bad things that were supposed to happen, they actually felt loved.

The church and the parents are the only two groups telling teens to abstain. (And that's often not the case either, with our morals and values constantly changing.) And let's face it—these groups are not the most sought-out and popular places where young people go for advice. Was it yours? Once again, remember your youth.

Parents and churches are also not doing the greatest job in what we teach about sex today. "If you do this, you'll either get pregnant or get AIDS, so stop it now." Is that the best we can do? Pregnancy is no longer a problem, with easy abortion available—and your kids don't even have to tell you. They also aren't going to tell you about the hidden apps on their cell phones that allow sexting to go on behind your back. And what happens when a cure for AIDS is ever found? Is sex then permissible?

The Bible never gives sexually transmitted disease as THE reason for abstinence.

We must be careful in claiming that disease is God's way of punishing sexually active people. What happened before STDs? Was premarital sex permissible then? Have we forgotten that the Bible still remains as God's best lesson book about sex, not AIDS?

Fear and guilt are the biggest weapons that churches use, especially with sex. We tell people that they'll feel really guilty if they have sex before marriage. That just isn't true; many end up feeling quite loved, accepted, secure, and close to someone for the first time in their lives. The *feeling* of guilt might never come—so we must emphasize the *fact* of guilt instead. There are many who don't feel guilty about a lot of things, but the fact remains that they are still guilty before God.

RESULTS: With the huge obsession of sex that has been implanted in their brains, we are beginning to see our younger generation buckle under that intense pressure. Sex is just way too difficult and heavy to handle, outside of marriage. That's why God put a fence around it—to protect us. He knows our limitations. It is one of His tender commandments that should be obeyed. As a result, we have a new generation of shallow, superficial, pleasure-seeking, empty, and angry people who sometimes actually will admit to themselves that they've been deceived and discarded.

Sex has been sold as the counterfeit for communication.

They've been taught that jumping into bed is the key to solving problems, when usually it's the way to create even bigger problems. They know how to open their legs but not their hearts. They know how to text but not to talk. They know social media but not spiritual conversation. Their decision to marry someone was based on pelvis or passion, not personality. Since the sex was great, they assumed their future would be. Now, they're realizing after all these years that they were dumped or duped.

Replacing a lifestyle of promiscuity with a lifestyle of monogamy is NOT easy. When you've had a long list of sexual partners, many are not content to have just one and only one, forever and ever. The wife compares her husband with the previous sexual partners she has had. The husband compares his wife in bed with the sexual satisfaction, positions, and performances of others that they had or viewed. Rarely will either one of them tell the other spouse (or their pastor) this vital information. All that is ever said is that one wants a divorce; people never get to the root cause. Church leaders must be willing to ask people more frequently about their sexual histories and habits. Again, pastors set the tone by their preaching here.

We have created a generation of liars who make promises that aren't true. They promised that they'd never leave. They promised they'd get married. They promised no one would get hurt. They agreed it would be a mutually consenting hook-up of casual sex, with no strings attached. They said whatever they needed to say to get what they wanted. Their lifestyle of lying must be replaced with a lifestyle of telling the truth in all the small and big things now. *We have created manipulators and exploiters who know how to masterfully use the opposite sex selfishly for their own interests.* They know all the lines and tricks. They have very little respect for their opposite sex. Sex has a way of making you feeling powerful over others, and we sinners will always love power.

We have created a generation of very bitter people who have been deceived and dumped for someone who is more muscular or bustier, skinnier or harder, smaller or bigger. The reasons are irrelevant; the pain is immense. When you willingly give your body in sexual intercourse to someone who throws you away for another person, it hurts. Millions of American boys and girls, men and women, are bitter to the core right now. They don't even know that they are deeply hurt. They were promised everything but got nothing. Or maybe they got a STD or AIDS. Some abstained from sex until marriage to avoid getting either, but then they got it from their spouse. They're mad at themselves, their one-night stands, their spouses, their boyfriends or girlfriends, or at the entire opposite sex right now. Some mistreat all men or women as a way of retaliating against one particular man or woman. The list could go on, and it does. We are buckling, and some are very bitter.

Casual sexual activity has left a bad taste in the mouths of some people, but for others it created a desire for even much more. As with any addiction, it takes more and more to satisfy us. What was initially sexually exciting has become downright boring. More is needed. A generation into fornication will soon lead to another generation of serial rapists, porn or sex addicts, and child molesters. We see this happening right now. So, what will you say to the sexually active?

The following examples are sermon suggestions, actual words, and counseling tips that can be used as you minister to the sexually active:

THE LIFE OF RAHAB: Joshua 2; 6; Hebrews 11:31; James 2:25; Matthew 1:5

Rahab was a promiscuous woman, we're told in Scripture. Today, we'd call her sexually active. She had many sexual partners and got quite a reputation. She didn't care to save sex for marriage and her body belonged to more than just one man. To Rahab, sex was not that sacred but instead it was rather casual and commonplace and frequent. We didn't recently invent sexual activity or curiosity

There are millions of Rahabs in our country, our churches, our schools, our workplaces, and our neighborhoods. We have men and women who have treated sex lightly and do not care to save it for their marriage mate. They come in all shapes and sizes, male and female, young and old alike. The reasons are just as numerous and various. It's everywhere today, and that might include church.

Rahab *was* a sexually active and loose woman, we're told. Past tense. Her sexual partners did not satisfy her soul. No creature could do what only the Creator could do and did do. She became a believer and abandoned that lifestyle. For the first time, she was free enough to care more about what God thought about her and not just what men thought. She changed. She put her trust in God, not man. And she then demonstrated that faith by helping some of God's people in their time of need. She laid her life on the line by doing so, and she was later rewarded by having her life spared. She is given very high grades and glowing recommendations. Rahab—the non-virgin, sexually active person—is then mightily used by God.

Are you a Rahab? Be honest here. Have you given away your virginity to others? Have you been sexually intimate with someone who is not your husband or wife? Would you like to be forgiven and changed, just like Rahab was? There's hope for you. Like Rahab, you need the Lord and can find Him. He is not far from you. The Lord loves you too much to allow you to lead a lifestyle of casual sex, like Rahab did. He knows it doesn't satisfy and He calls you to Himself now. He'll satisfy your needs. No matter what your past is like, you can be forgiven, restored, useful, and pure.

Your life is not over when your virginity is. Ask Rahab! God takes bodies that have been sexually used by others and doesn't hold that against them any longer. God forgave Rahab's sin like He forgives all sins: by the blood of Jesus. Isn't that the reason why God chose the color red for that cord in the window that saved them?

Rahab and her family were the only ones God spared in Jericho. Good news came from the life of Rahab. God chose this sexually active woman to be one of the ancestors of Jesus, His Son. What hope and encouragement there is for us, any of us, all of us, regardless of our past. For those who have made a lifetime of mistakes or just one mistake when it comes to sex, Rahab is your second chance. She is that symbol of hope for you. She tells you that God has bigger and better plans for you.

THE LIFE OF JACOB AND ESAU: Genesis 25–35

Jacob was a man who knew what he wanted and usually found a way to get it. At times, he was downright devious and deceitful. He lied and tricked others often, into doing what he wanted them to do. We see that practice with Laban in Genesis 31 and we see what he did with Isaac in Genesis 27. Jacob's life was not very honest, clean, or pure before he met God.

One of his more notable and questionable tricks was reported in Genesis 25. It involved his brother. Esau was the older of the two and thus, he was entitled to a birthright which gave him twice the inheritance of Jacob (Deut. 21:17) and also the higher blessing of his father (Gen. 27:35). Jacob gave his hungry brother some food in exchange for the birthright. It was not a fair trade but it was mutually agreed upon—mutually consenting adults, as we would say today.

In our text, the Scriptures assign more blame to Esau who "despised his birthright." He valued something so important, so lightly. He was willing to give away something so permanent for something that was so temporary. For one moment of physical pleasure to indulge his flesh, he gave up his sacred birthright.

There are many Esaus in America. So many people give away their birthright and virginity for just one moment of physical or sexual pleasure. They put very little value on their virginity or sexuality, which are gifts and birthrights given to them by God. So many boys and girls and men and women are giving away something so important for something so fleeting, just like Esau did. Esau only thought of the present, not the future. He wanted to satisfy his urgent physical desires and he had to have that food, right there and then.

Esau needed help in battling temptations and winning those battles. Might you, too? He didn't consider the consequences of his actions; and when he finally did see what he did and what was done to him, he got angry for years on end and held a big grudge (Gen. 27:41). Esau finally got the chance to meet up with Jacob in Genesis 33, but few get that chance to meet the Jacobs in their own lives and confront them. Might you be holding a grudge today against someone who wronged you?

You might be an Esau today, but you might also be a Jacob. You asked for something that did not belong to you; you wanted something that was not yours. You acted dishonorably toward a member of the opposite (or same) sex. You did whatever it took to get his or her birthright, virginity, and innocence. You took advantage of the moment and the person. You've done it that one time, or maybe more than one time. Might you sexually see yourself in Jacob here?

Are you a manipulator who engineers your situations to get what you want, like Jacob did? How many people have you tricked? How many birthrights have you stolen? How many bodies have you used? How many hearts have you broken? How many families have you ruined, just like Jacob did here? When will you stop your lying and manipulating? It's hard to look in the mirror now, as a result.

Jacob met his match, finally. He met God Himself in a wrestling match, we're told. God won the match and changed Jacob's life. God didn't hurt Jacob for hurting other people; instead, He humbled him. He helped Jacob to see that his lifestyle of lying, using, deceiving, and hurting people was finally over. What a relief it was for Jacob. After his conversion, he is a different man. Might you need to have your own wrestling match with God right now and surrender to Him?

THE LIFE OF DANIEL: The Book of Daniel and Ezekiel 14:14, 20

Daniel stands out as one of the finest young men in the Old Testament. While still young, he is taken captive to a foreign country and exposed to strong temptations and challenges which did not get the best of him. He won the war within. He was the cream of the crop in terms of ability, personality, integrity, intelligence, and appearance. He had it all, and Nebuchadnezzar wanted Daniel to be his own personal servant. To that end, he gave Daniel whatever seemed good and made him happy. Having the king write you a blank check is quite an honor for Daniel.

Like any teenager, food was a top priority. This was good food, not fast food. Daniel was told to eat anything he wanted and all he wanted, as long as he would be happy. The menu was tempting and attractive but Daniel refused this food—only because God did. God had forbidden these types of food, and Daniel purposed in his heart to obey God in this. Daniel dared to be different and decided to refrain from doing what any younger (or even older) person would normally do.

There are a lot of very attractive and tasty temptations for you, as a Daniel. Many look good and appeal to your fleshly desires and appetites. And there are a whole lot of Nebuchadnezzars out there who are tempting you to partake in some experiences or behaviors that might defile your body and disappoint your God.

Sex is one of those. God says you can enjoy all you want—with your marriage mate. Everyone tells us to do this right now, instead of waiting for (or in addition to) your spouse. Enjoy all you want as long as you are protected, right? You might have some Nebuchadnezzars in your life who do their best to tempt you. Who might yours be today? It is extremely difficult to stay sexually pure and stand firm when society tells us the opposite.

Many have given in. Maybe you did. Probably you did. You thought that the law of the land was more important than God's law. You didn't want to be punished or ridiculed for being a virgin. You gave into peer pressure and you already ordered from the sex menu selections right there in front of you.

You didn't have to, though. You could have been Daniel who didn't order from the menu. Sure it wasn't easy but God rewarded him, didn't He? God nourished Daniel and his friends in a different and better way, in Daniel 1:15–21. They turned out to be better off than those who defiled themselves with the tasty food. Isn't that so typical of God, whose ways are higher and better than all our ways?

THE WOMAN AT THE WELL: John 4:1–42

Jesus is the friend of sinners, and that happens to include sexual sinners. God does not put them in a separate category, even though people put them there. Sin is sin—whether it be sexual or nonsexual.

This was not the first or last conversation that Jesus had with sexually active people who were all around him. There's the woman in Luke 7:36–50. Jesus welcomed her, even though the religious people shunned her. Jesus does the exact same here with this woman at the well. Jesus knew her sexual mistakes beforehand. Her loose lifestyle didn't scare Him away. We have much to learn from His example as a church and as individual believers here. We really do! This woman had five previous husbands, but Jesus didn't get all upset or intimidated by her past. She was living again with someone who was not her husband, much like what's happening in our own society. Jesus ministers to her and converts her. He told her she would never thirst again. He knew everything (and everyone) she had ever done and still, He went out to her. He ministered to her, and then through her. Others came to believe in Jesus because of her.

Can you believe it? A sexually active person becomes a very effective evangelist to her entire community, as a result!

A lot of people have a hard time with that, sometimes because of their own sexual guilt and sometimes because of their own self-righteousness. Whether you are a spectator or a participant in the game of sex, you might think God could never use a person who has been sexually active in his or her past. You are wrong. In a similar story of a prodigal son who was living a life with few boundaries like this woman, we read that the father eagerly welcomed him back home, in Luke 15:13–30.

Regardless of whether you're male or female, younger or older, Jesus does not disqualify you based on how many sexual partners you might have had in your lifetime. He offers you the same kind of new life He offered this woman at the well. Will you work alongside Him, since He already knows everything you've done? You won't scare Him away, even though you might scare religious people away with your confession. Jesus knows why you have done what you did, and offers you the kind of living water that will satisfy you during this life.

THE CONTRAST BETWEEN DAVID AND SOLOMON:
1 Kings 11:1–13; 2 Samuel 7; 12; 22–23; Nehemiah 13:23–27

Both of these men sinned against the Lord. Like father, like son. Both fell into sexual temptation. However, there's a big difference between David and Solomon, stated in 1 Kings 11. David made a mistake, a big mistake, a one-time mistake. He sinned with Bathsheba. But once he was rebuked, he confessed and renounced his sin. We read of his heart's agony in Psalms 32 and 51. His heart was once again right with the Lord and he stayed that way. David is described as "a man after God's own heart" in Acts 13:22. The same Nathan who rebuked him in 2 Samuel 12 also reassured him that God would never take His love away from him, in 2 Samuel 7:15–16. David believed it.

So can you. If you've sinned like David did, hear me as your Nathan in both rebuking yet reassuring you. Maybe you've only been listening to your own heart condemn you for your time with your secret Bathsheba no one knows about. Maybe you've justified it in your heart and feel no guilt. It's not working anymore. Now for the first time, you're hearing how God wants to restore you back to Him.

Solomon's heart was far different, though, and he didn't listen to God's voice. We're told his heart was turned away from the Lord because of the many women for whom he loved and lusted. His was not a one-time indiscretion but a lifetime of mistakes. Solomon held fast to his sin instead. His wives turned his heart toward other gods. His life turned out to be quite different. As the number of wives, lovers, and sexual partners increased, his love for God began to decrease. He was so obsessed with the opposite sex that he forgot all about God. Is this you today?

Notice that God emphasizes and highlights the heart. He looks at your heart. Where is your heart today? Is it preoccupied with the opposite sex, like Solomon? Or is it broken with sorrow over a sexual mistake you made with your Bathsheba?

In our society, we have many more Solomons than we have Davids. Instead of a one-time mistake (or partner) like David had, many make sex a full-time pursuit. They become slaves to sexual passion or partners, just like Solomon.

Which are you? He knows who and how many and how strong that sexual urge is. He knows your heart and whether it is already hardened like Solomon's or softened like David's. Today is when you can switch from being a Solomon to a David.

JUDAH AND TAMAR, IN CONTRAST TO JOSEPH AND POTIPHAR'S WIFE: Genesis 38–39

It's no coincidence that there's an interruption to the narrative of Joseph's life in the book of Genesis. In chapter 37, he is unjustly sold into slavery by his brothers; then in chapter 39, he is unjustly put into prison by a woman. Chapter 38 seems to be strangely inserted! This chapter is here to show why Joseph and his family ended up in Egypt. Had they all remained in Canaan, the sons would have all married Canaanite women just like Judah did in Chapter 38. God's people would have lost their distinctiveness as a people. He calls us to be separated and set apart.

We also see how two different men handle the exact same sexual temptation. That temptation is one that many men and women have today: to be sexually involved with someone who is not your marriage partner. Some identify here with Tamar, some will identify with Judah, and some will identify with Joseph.

Which Bible character here intrigues you the most? Who do you identify with?

Here's the story and background. Judah was the fourth son of Leah and Jacob. He married a Canaanite woman named Shuah and had three sons. In time, Judah got a wife for one of his sons named Er, whose name was Tamar. Due to sin on the part of Er, and then his brother Onan, they were both put to death.

Shelah was the only son left and Tamar should have married him, eventually. Judah was supposed to arrange this so she waited and waited. Finally, she took matters into her own hands. She disguised herself as a prostitute and waited where she knew Judah would soon be walking. She also knew that Judah would probably give into her sexual temptation. Well, he did. Judah did not know it was her, and he had his one-night stand with Tamar.

Three months later, Judah learns that Tamar is pregnant. Not knowing that he is the father, he orders her punished until he discovers that it is his child that she bears. Judah also admits his guilt in not previously giving his son Shelah as a husband for Tamar. Doesn't this sound like one of our modern reality TV shows?

There are boys and men who act just like Judah here. They have sex with someone else and give into temptation just as quickly and easily as Judah did. And like Judah, you'll find them in church living a kind of life different than the one they live the rest of the week. They are men who are hypocrites, insisting that the woman be punished for her sexual immorality while he secretly continues his escapades. They have secrets no one knows, they think. Might you be Judah in our text? In which way do you identify with him?

There are girls and women who act like Tamar here. They have sex outside of marriage. They actively seduce, or passively allow themselves to be seduced by men. It might be a boyfriend, it might be an affair, or it might be a friend or stranger. You have your reasons, like Tamar did. She wanted something more permanent than sex; she wanted a child. That might be the last thing you want but you still use a man to get something you want or feel you need in your life. You use sex or people to get something else.

Maybe that's the reason that Potiphar's wife tried to seduce Joseph in chapter 39. Maybe it was her lusting for his younger or harder flesh. Regardless, she was wrong. She tried to seduce Joseph, just like Tamar seduced Judah in chapter 38. But Joseph was not Judah; he did not give in. He resisted and ran away instead.

Who said the Bible was old-fashioned? You find real lives and temptations here. You find some who fall, but some who stand their ground in the battle for sexual purity. You find some Josephs who say "How can I do this and sin against God?" and others who give into temptation when put in front of them. Which will you be, Joseph or Judah? May you decide today to be just like Joseph!

6

ABORTION

Words can't describe the joy—or the pain—of seeing your very first baby. Most women are totally overwhelmed with joy, but some feel the exact opposite emotion. Sally told everybody it was her first but she knew that she was lying. This baby reminded her of the other two that she had aborted many years ago. She thought she had forgotten the whole thing, but this helpless little baby brought back some very powerful and painful memories. When people told her that her baby looked just like her, she couldn't help but wonder if her other ones would have looked like her too. She's having a tough time trying to forget her abortions.

When I asked Fred what was stopping him from becoming a Christian, he looked at me as if I knew his secret. He got visibly angry and quickly irritated. He mumbled something about killing somebody. When I asked him about this, he told me he got a girl pregnant, made her get an abortion, and then left her. He didn't feel guilty for leaving his girlfriend but he did feel guilty for aborting his baby. He carried this guilt for years and couldn't rid himself of it. He wept like a child as we spoke. I told him that God could forgive his sin, but he insisted that his sin was far too great for God to forgive. To this day, I wonder if Fred is still tortured by guilt. I wonder how often his anger erupts at people much like it burst out upon me.

Barb's relationship with her husband was more than she could ever ask, except for just one thing. She did not enjoy sex. She hated it. Why? In her mind, sex meant death. When she got an abortion as a teenager, she knew she was doing something wrong. Because of sex, someone died—someone who shouldn't have. Barb has a very hard time enjoying sex with her husband now because she doesn't think she deserves to. So, she's learned to simply endure it and not enjoy it.

Mother of the Year? The award that Mrs. Bailey got from church only made matters worse. She felt that she deserved a crown of thorns instead. After all, a "Mother of the Year" doesn't kill her own grandchild, does she? But she did. She insisted that terminating the pregnancy was the best solution for her teenage daughter, and even drove her daughter to the abortion clinic. Ever since then, the family fun times changed. Life is different at home. Mother and daughter became cold toward each other and don't talk together as much as they used to. By the way, her daughter didn't come with her when she got the award.

When you counsel or preach about abortion, don't forget the millions of victims who are still alive. They sit in your church and hear your sermons. What about the doctors and nurses who performed those abortions and have a hard time sleeping now? What about the close friends who drove their friend to the hospital? What about those who advised or insisted on it? What about the grandparents who paid for it? What about the men who deeply grieve that they had no say in the death of the little one they wanted to love? What about the men who made sure it happened? What about the younger or older women who physically suffer now as a result of their abortion but can't tell anyone why? These numbers reach into the millions.

I quoted the wrong number for years as I spoke at pro-life rallies and gave powerful speeches describing abortions. I talked about the procedures and the babies but forgot to calculate in, or speak to, those abortion victims who still live. I am so grateful the Lord drew some to come for counseling afterward, in spite of my harsh words. As a result, you'll never hear me speak about abortion again without my offering hope and forgiveness for these walking but wounded abortion victims.

Preachers get so caught up with the little people that we tend to forget about the big people affected by abortion.

Yes, I know that millions of men and women have no remorse but only relief. But when some finally come to the Lord and grow in Him, they feel that need to ask for forgiveness and grieve over their unborn child. Church leaders will need to pick up the pieces of broken hearts as they count the number of broken babies. When they hear the Lord tell them that "you are the one," will they also hear you say that "the Lord has taken away your sin" (2 Sam. 12:7, 13) when their sin is forgiven by the blood of Jesus Christ? When it comes to abortion, we've also been given a ministry to comfort those who mourn (Isa. 61:1–7)! *We have gotten so wrapped up in the issue that we have forgotten the individuals.* Do you have any compassion in your heart (or sermons) for the people who have already chosen abortion?

Maybe you see nothing wrong with abortion and cling to a "pro-choice" stance instead. You are doing your congregation and community a huge disservice in presenting neither truth nor grace. Regardless of what you believe, God is much bigger. We can try to suppress or erase sin, but God has His way of getting us to listen.

Some of these women and men are reminded daily. They go to the mall, see playful children, and remember. They see baby furniture in the stores and remember. They hear a friend is pregnant and remember. They hear a vacuum cleaner or wash the kitchen knives and remember. They don't trust men. They are angry at women. They go to a child's birthday party and remember. They have nightmare visitations from the aborted child. They walk on by the church nursery without peeking inside. They witness an infant dedication or baptism and wonder. They worry that their other children will find out one day. They have a secret to hide and a sin that needs to be wept over (Luke 7:36–50). They need your help.

The biggest mistake we make is in telling these women to just get over their abortions and try to forget about them. Is that what you tell a mother who has had a miscarriage? Wouldn't that be insensitive and cruel? A woman has an attachment to her unborn baby. That's a good thing and that's a God thing. We must allow and encourage her to truly grieve for the child she will never see and also grieve with her. Do not trivialize this grief process and ask her to just get on with life. Don't tell her to try and forget. Don't give such insensitive advice! Unfortunately, that's what most people now advise. Instead, encourage her to grieve or weep out loud. God understands the need for a mother to grieve for her lost child (Isa. 49:15; Zech. 12:10), so why don't we? Read Genesis 37 and how Jacob grieves over his son Joseph whom he thought had died. Go through 2 Samuel and watch David weep over the death of his children. Read 1 Samuel 30:1–6 to see how parents weep at the loss of their family. See Matthew 2:16–18 and imagine yourself losing your child this way. First Thessalonians 4:13–18 describes the need to grieve. Go through the Gospels and notice the grief that people had over the death of their children that they asked Jesus to heal or to raise. Jesus knew the pain his mother was enduring as He told John to take care of her (John 19:26–27) after His death on the cross. The Scriptures are full of examples of our need to grieve.

Abortion isn't easy to forget, because a child is not easy to forget!

Abortion is a death without a funeral. No flowers are given in memory; no friends come to express sympathy. You go alone and suffer alone. Those who you thought were your friends aren't there for you. Ultimately, you're left alone. There is no support.

Grief is even more difficult to resolve when you have had ambivalent feelings toward your baby. You didn't want the fetus but you did want your baby. You loved the baby but hated it for what it would do to your reputation, career, graduation, family, or future. You're confused and conflicted. Now, it's too late.

What makes the grief process more unbearable is that you contributed to their death. Deep grief is multiplied and intensified by real guilt. Speak to parents who feel responsible for the *accidental* death of their child. They die hourly and daily. Imagine how much greater the burden is for people who chose, paid for, performed, or advised abortion. This was intentional, though, and not accidental.

Not only are they angry at themselves but they're also quite upset at the opposite sex. We have an entire generation of women who have become extremely bitter and hateful toward men. Oh, they won't tell you the reason for their pent-up anger, but sometimes it is deeply internalized and widely generalized. She gave up her baby to keep *him*—only to lose him to another woman after he abandoned her. She is left all alone and she hates all men now. She doesn't even see that now and never will.

Yes, I know that most men are supportive of a woman's right to choose, which translates into their right to irresponsibly impregnate. But for those men who choose to accept their feelings, they suffer too. For either sex, the loss of a life is hard to cope with. Like the baby, his voice is never heard. How would you react if you felt totally and legally helpless while someone else signed the papers that ended the life of your child? How would you treat this person now? Some men end up generalizing their anger toward all women because of what one woman did.

Some men hesitate to become emotionally involved with, or attached to, their unborn baby since he is never sure if his partner might abort this baby. She can always change her mind and abort. Since he doesn't become concerned for the child before birth, the same pattern carries on after birth. They never see this.

I also know parents who are extremely overprotective of their children, since they're trying to make up for the loss of their aborted one and eradicate their guilt by pouring everything they now have into their surviving child. They never see it.

God does not leave the guilty unpunished. He punishes the children and their children for the sin of the fathers to the third and fourth generation (Ex. 34:7b). Their innocent blood cries out to Him for justice (Gen. 4:1–11). Even if abortion were outlawed tomorrow, you would still need the rest of your life to minister to the millions who have already been emotionally affected by it.

You don't have to preach a whole sermon on this topic but you should carefully insert wisely worded sentences or paragraphs to draw people out. You could pick texts that are directly relevant. See Deuteronomy 30:19–20; Psalms 8; 22:9–10; 139; Isaiah 44:2–4; 49:1; Jeremiah 1:5; Matthew 2:16–18. But there are many texts that indirectly speak to other abortion victims. People will take notice.

The following examples are sermon suggestions, actual words, and counseling tips that can be used as you minister to abortion victims:

THE LIFE OF PAUL: Acts 7:59–8:3; 9:1–31; 1 Timothy 1:15–16; Philippians 3:12–14

Paul knew that he was responsible for the deaths of many people. He participated, approved of, and signed the execution orders as his daily job. Upon conversion, that memory surely stayed with him. He calls himself "the chief of sinners," but he also knew that God forgave him for executing innocent people. He could not bring back the body of Stephen or other Christians he had executed, and he had to live with that memory as he saw some families in the churches to whom he ministered.

There are lots of people like Paul today. They feel just like Paul. Some actually did what Paul did: They killed someone and now have to live with that haunting memory. An abortion is an execution; and many, like Paul, have signed the execution papers, given their consent, or even performed them. Women, men, roommates, nurses, doctors, parents, and grandparents—the list can go on. How many Stephens have you executed? What reminds or haunts you of what you did, allowed, advised, or insisted upon? You have a secret. Are you a secret Paul?

God forgave Paul, in Christ. The blood of Jesus cleansed him from all sin, even the sin of taking the life of another. He wants to do the same for you and your abortion. Might you live with that nagging memory today? Does this topic make you sad today? I understand your pain, but I also know how to relieve that pain. Paul consciously chose to remember that his decision to take lives was forgiven by God and that Jesus paid for that mistake. Paul had to try to forget the painful memories of the past and press on toward the future for which God called him. Will you do that? Paul was totally blown away and amazed at God's forgiveness. Will you be? Might this be the day when you're set free, just like Paul was?

THE LIFE OF DAVID: *2 Samuel 11–24; Psalms 32; 51*

God held David responsible for the death of his firstborn son due to his unlawful sexual union with Bathsheba. Indirectly, it was *his* fault that the boy died—but it was his fault directly that Uriah died. He neatly tried to dispose of someone who he thought would ruin the plans he had made for himself and Bathsheba. And that's not all; by the end of the story, David was partially responsible for the death of his other sons, wasn't he? One moment of passion and panic ended in the death of a lot of innocent people.

The same is true today of abortion. Whether you directly or indirectly were responsible for the neat disposal of someone else, it haunts you too. You try and muffled the sound but you hear Nathan say "you are the one." You might be reminded in the smallest of ways, at times you least expect it. However, David listened to his Nathan and confessed and repented of his sin. Will you listen and confess, too? David's life was not over because of what he did. He found the forgiveness that God offers through Jesus Christ. All of the guilt, grief, and shame were taken away and replaced with the joy of salvation.

THE CRIMINAL ON THE CROSS: *Luke 23:39–43*

For the very first time in his life, a convicted murderer finally feels the full force of what he had done. He admitted he was wrong—dead wrong. And there on that lonely cross was a man who wondered if God could forgive him. God answered his question with the presence of another man who committed no sin and murdered no one. His whole life was devoted to doing for others. Listen to Jesus say to this man, "Today, you'll be with me in Paradise." Can you imagine how that felt to him?

The same can be true for you. Maybe for the first time in your life, you feel the full force of some of the things you've done in your life. You've been trying to deny it but then all of a sudden, God puts something or someone in your presence. You hear your friend is pregnant and remember the baby you'll never see, touch, or hold. You see a baby stroller in the mall. You've been telling yourself you had good reasons for what you did, just like the man on the cross. What about that abortion that you had? That you insisted that she have? Have you also realized the full force of what you did? Why not? When you do, come also to Jesus—just like the man on the cross did. Today can be that new start and a peaceful conscience as you walk with Jesus no matter what you've done before. There is no sin too big for God.

THE EXAMPLE OF SARAI AND ABRAHAM: Genesis 16

Abraham and Sarai loved each other deeply, but had a problem and wanted a quick fix to solve it. Hagar enters the picture and the problem seems to go away and be solved . . . but it wasn't. They end up hurting a lot of innocent people in their rush to fix a problem their way and not God's way.

There are lots of people today like Abraham and Sarai. Their problem is called a pregnancy and they want a quick fix to solving it. So they decide to abort, and the problem seems to go away and be solved . . . but it isn't. Just like Abraham and Sarai, we view sex lightly and then we try to take care of it quickly.

Today, unborn babies become Hagars in our lives. They are bad memories of quick decisions. And we try to do to them what Sarai did to her: We throw them out and try to erase the memories. But Hagar hung around and didn't go away. Neither do the memories of abortion. Might you be Abraham or Sarai today? Might you have a Hagar who reminds you daily of what you once decided to do? It might be a nightmare or a baby's name that no one knows about. God can help you.

JOSEPH AND HIS BROTHERS: Genesis 37–50 (42:21–24; 44:30–34)

Knowing or even thinking that you're responsible for someone else's death can bring such guilt, shame, and sorrow that it lingers for an entire lifetime. It did with Joseph's brothers! They wanted him out of the way and did their best to get rid of him. They devised a great plan and thought it was failproof and foolproof. Joseph was gone with one decision. Poof, he was gone! Abortion can do the same thing to you. Thinking that you are responsible for someone else's death, especially from your own flesh and blood, is hard. It gnaws away at you, like it did with Joseph's brothers, for a very long time. But our story would not be complete without Genesis 45 and 50. Notice the deep relief, joy, weeping, and kissing when they realize that they could be forgiven for their actions! Do you need this forgiveness today?

Joseph knew that they intended to harm him but God used it for good for the saving of many lives. You can use your abortion decision for the saving of many lives in the future. As you feel that forgiveness that comes only from God, you'll want to share that great news with others who also need to know.

THE EXAMPLE OF PETER: Mark 14:66–72; 16:7; John 21; Galatians 2:11–14

Peter is not the first to compromise his faith out of fear. He's not the first to abandon his morals when the panic button gets pushed. He turns out to be inconsistent and he runs away from what he knew was right to do. Many of us act just like Peter did two thousand years ago. In our homes, at school and at work—we compromise for a variety of reasons. We do it daily.

Many of us compromise on the issue called abortion. We end up denying our Lord by our attitudes and actions, too. We get scared, like Peter did, and we run away from what we know we should do. We, like Peter, say of our newly conceived unborn child: "I never knew him." We betray our unborn baby and also our Lord.

But that doesn't change the reality that we did know him or her, and that we still do. The memory doesn't go away and sooner or later, we need to do what Peter did. He broke down and wept. You might need to weep bitterly, just like Peter did. Some have not done that yet but should. Nothing would be more healing to your soul.

Imagine Peter's guilt when he did nothing at all as Jesus was led to His death.

I know the guilt you feel as you let your baby be led to his or her death.

But I also know the freedom you can feel when Jesus forgives you for it. After His resurrection, Jesus made sure that Peter would *not* wallow away in guilt, depression, and self-condemnation for the rest of his life. He doesn't want you to do that either. Maybe you've been doing that, and maybe today will be different.

Jesus made a personal visit to Peter, and wants to make one with you, too. God invited Peter to fellowship and work with Him, even after what he did. The same is true for you—even after what you did and how you denied that little one and let him or her be executed. Jesus forgave this betrayal and betrayer. He can do the same for you and He will forgive you and then use you for His own glory.

THE EXAMPLE OF REBEKAH: Genesis 27

Rebekah made a decision she thought would be in the best interest of her child and for herself. It didn't seem like that bad of an idea at the time. She never dreamed of what might happen as a result of that quick decision. Did you know she never saw her child again for the rest of her life? She surely didn't even consider that might happen as she did what she did. She had no idea.

This scene is repeated every day in America with abortion. Every day there are Rebekahs who decide to do something they *think* is in everyone's best interests. They decide to abort, and they too will never see their child. Imagine how much Rebekah missed Jacob. Imagine the guilt she felt for tricking Isaac and causing him so much sorrow and pain. Imagine how angry she got at herself for her plan and for what she had done.

Are you like Rebekah? Do you wish you could take it all back and have your baby back? Do you miss your child? Do you regret your abortion today? Are you angry at yourself? Did you ever dream you'd feel the way you do now? The guilt, the loss, the pain, the ache. This is an ache that you need to give to God now.

THE EXAMPLE OF ABRAM AND SARAI: Genesis 12:10–20; 20:1–2

In order to save his own skin, Abram (who was later renamed Abraham) did something that boggles our mind here. He betrayed someone he cared for very deeply out of panic, fear, convenience, or selfishness. Who knows? Maybe it was all of them.

Imagine how Sarai felt during all of this. He put her into danger and put his own interests first and foremost, not caring what might happen to her.

Before we get angry at Abraham, let's take the log out of our own eyes. Let's not judge this man too quickly, since men and women do the same today when it comes to choosing abortion. Whatever the reason is, we put ourselves first while the other person is left out of the decision. Maybe you were not consulted; or maybe the decision to abort was handed down by your boyfriend, girlfriend, or parents. You were told what to do, just like Sarai. It was out of your hands.

And you went to the abortion chambers instead of Pharoah's chambers. You went alone. Where was your Abraham? Where did he or they go when you needed someone? Where are the men who leave their precious Sarais to save their own skin? Where are the women who never consult with their partners but decide on their own about the fate or future of another? Before we pass judgment on Abraham, let us remember that we become much like Abraham with an abortion decision.

THE EXAMPLE OF LOT AND THE LEVITE: Genesis 19; Judges 19

As you read this story, you become horrified at what is really happening. Just the idea of offering up someone else's life as a cultural custom is mind-boggling. But before you think our culture is so advanced, consider our culture and abortion.

We are not that much different from those people in Genesis 19 and Judges 19. We offer up our own flesh and blood— our unborn children—and call it a "no-brainer." Like a cultural custom, it's somewhat expected and totally acceptable. And unfortunately, many of our unborn sons and daughters get abused and butchered—just like the concubine in Judges 19. It is not a pretty sight, is it? Have you acted like Lot here? Who have you offered up as a cultural norm? Have you given into the temptation that the Levite did and now regret it? Are you here in this story but in a more modern-day setting with abortion? Might we be guilty of doing the same?

THE EXAMPLE OF EVE: *Genesis 3; John 8:44; Hebrews 3:13*

Satan is a master at telling lies and half-truths. He is the father of lies and tells you only what he wants you to know, and usually what you want to hear. He tricks you and he chooses carefully selected words to trip you up. He did that to Eve and Adam into making a decision that they (and we) would regret the rest of their (and our) lives. He is a master at using words to deceive.

Abortion is an example. Both we, and he, use very pretty words to disguise ugly things—"reproductive rights," "termination of a pregnancy," "doing what we want to do with our own body," "unwanted tissue," "cells that adhere to a uterine wall," "products of conception," "the freedom to be female." The list could go on. These words work, just as Satan's words did with Eve. He told them it would be in their best interests and she listened, just like we do. These are half-truths and lies, also.

Like Eve, we make decisions that we regret for the rest of our lives. We give in. Satan is so tricky, and sin is so deceitful. So we should not be so judgmental toward those women (or men) who listen to Satan and decide to abort. They got tricked by fancy tricky words, just like Eve did and just like we do.

But God had the final words with Eve, and He wants to do the same with you. Watch God give Eve a new wardrobe of animal skins—a symbol of Jesus's death in the far future, which alone can cover her sin and also your sin.

THE EXAMPLE OF SOLOMON'S WISDOM WITH THE WOMEN: *1 Kings 3*

These two women remind me of how men and women deal with abortion. Women and men fight over the unborn baby. One wants it while the other doesn't. One wants to care for it while the other couldn't care less. Now imagine the anger and hatred that the woman who wanted the baby would feel toward the woman who wanted to injure the baby. Do you think they would ever be best buddies in life?

Men and women fight just like this. We have huge issues of mistrust and anger, seething toward each other. Maybe you have issues with other men or women—maybe due to this topic of abortion. It caused quite a fight or breakup, didn't it? You'll never forget that conversation.

I see another story here about abortion. Sometimes people act and feel like the one woman who didn't care about the baby. Then after the abortion, they act and feel like the other woman who did want the baby. They have two minds and conflicting thoughts fighting over the same baby, just like we have two women fighting here over the same baby. Have you had that happen to you? You seem like two different people about your abortion and over your child you'll never see. You wonder if you're going crazy. Maybe it's time you consult with One who Scripture says is greater than Solomon—and his name is Jesus. He is the only wise God and can help you have peace. He brings order out of confusion and chaos.

THE EXAMPLE OF GOVERNMENT, LAW, AND CAPITAL PUNISHMENT: *Romans 13:1–5; Genesis 9:6; Matthew 2:16–18; Exodus 1:15–2:10; Acts 4*

Laws are meant to protect the innocent and punish the guilty. However, sometimes they do the opposite. You might have felt that the law seemed to protect the guilty and punish the innocent. We see injustice and it really hurts.

Today, that's true with abortion. Unborn babies are innocent; the laws are supposed to protect them but they don't. It's open game on them. At least there were cities of refuge in the Old Testament you could run to and be safe there. The womb used to be a city of refuge for unborn children. But that city of refuge has instead become a carving station, or a suction machine, or a lethal injection.

Laws like those in Matthew 2 and Exodus 1 legalized the taking of little lives. Today, we too rationalize that if something is legal, it is ethical. A lot of people don't think it through but blindly follow. They do what the law allows and they have an abortion, or they advise or insist that someone else have it. Maybe they perform them.

However, you don't have to give in and be like them. The midwives didn't. The apostles didn't. They knew there was a higher law to follow.

We should not be so disgusted by people who have had abortions. After all, they followed the law of the land. Sheep foolishly follow and that is what God calls us. Let's have compassion on the sheep who follow the law and decide to abort.

7

SEXUAL ASSAULT AND RAPE

The wind, snow, and freezing temperatures set new records for the area; Betty was so glad to be warmly nestled in front of the family room fireplace with a big mug of hot coffee. She hated to get up and answer that doorbell, and allow that blast of blizzard cold air to invade her warm home.

As she squinted with her eyes to look outside through the frosted glass near the door, she saw a man on her front porch desperately trying to warm his hands. She also saw a car with the hood propped up there on the road in front of her house. She figured he needed help. As a good Christian, she opened the door.

He only needed to use her phone and mumbled something about calling a nearby gas station that could fix his car so he could be back on his way to work in a few minutes. His cell phone was dead and it would only take a quick second.

But it seemed like a lifetime instead.

He didn't want to use her phone; instead, he wanted to use her body. He raped her right there in front of the family-room fireplace. And when he was done, he left in the same car that needed no repair at all. Her home was invaded, her trust was destroyed, her body was violated, her fear had begun, her home got colder, and her life was changed.

Her husband was out of town and the kids were at school. Her neighbors were not home and her friends were all at work. So, she called her pastor—after she took a very long hot shower and tried to wash off the shame she felt. She got dressed and went to church, hoping to find words of comfort and hope from her pastor. Surely, he would know what to say.

But he didn't.

He asked her why she would allow a total stranger in her house. He asked her if she knew him. He asked her what she was wearing. He asked her if she might have done anything to encourage him. He asked her if she screamed for help and why not. He asked her if she tried to fight back or if she got the license plate. Twenty questions—somehow she was the one who was now on trial. But the pastor never asked her if she was hurt, how she felt, or if she wanted to cry.

And then (as pastors love to do) his sermon began. He told her how foolish she was for letting the man into her house and how she should have screamed for help or beat him off of her. He also told her that this world is evil and that we should not put our trust in man but only in God. He told her that God allowed it to happen and that He would bring good out of the whole experience and to trust Him to do that in due time. And then, her pastor said that she needed to forgive this man for what he had done to her and that she should not harbor any anger in her heart toward him. He told her that bitterness is just as much of a sin as rape is. And he told her that she needed to get over it, ask God for strength, and get on with her life. He told her that good Christians aren't sup-posed to hold grudges.

The pastor, of course, did all the preaching and talking, while Betty just listened.

After a quick prayer, Betty went back home. She was actu-ally now more dazed, confused, and depressed than she was right after her rape. What just happened? *She did not expect her time with her pastor to be as humiliating and degrading as her time with her rapist.* Instead of opening his heart toward her, he pointed his finger toward her by telling her what she had done wrong. She came to him to be comforted but got condemned. He didn't take away her pain but only added to it. As preachers and pastors, we must upgrade our skills in knowing about rape. We really can botch it up badly here, if we are not careful.

You can unintentionally and emotionally rape your own members in the comfort of your own church office.

Rape is not something that will typically make it on your church's prayer list on Wednesday nights or midweek service. No one activates the prayer chain for church women who get raped. You never hear a sermon on it and never have a church support group for these ladies. It's kept silent, and church folks aren't supposed to talk about this.

MILLIONS: Rape is the most rapidly growing, yet most under-reported, crime in America. Best estimates are that a million women are actually raped each year in America. While 300,000 rapes are reported yearly in the USA, note that two-thirds of rapes are never reported at all. Preachers rant and rave about the million women each year who have abortions, but selectively ignore the million men who rape each year. Why do we usually tend to speak up against women but rarely speak up for women? Is a woman less important than a fetus? *Why do some preachers speak up for the million abortion victims but say nothing about the million rape victims?* They speak against the women who abort but never speak up for the women who are raped. Once again, we are quite too selective about our sins—especially our sexual sins.

Rape happens when a person is forced or coerced into any type of sexual contact with another person. That is a broad but good definition to remember.

One in six women has experienced an attempted or completed rape. The vast majority are women who are under age thirty. Almost all of them know the attacker. A woman is sexually assaulted every two minutes in the USA. One out of every three females will be sexually assaulted by rape, attempted rape, non-consensual touching, molestation, or childhood sexual abuse at some point in her lifetime.

A woman receives a salary increase from her boss who is not only generous with his money but also with his compliments about her work and also her body. She is surprised and does not know how to respond. After all, church tells us to turn the other cheek, right? She is promoted to work directly under him and is given an even larger increase. She needs the money since her husband left her. One night, her boss begins to unbutton her blouse when they are all alone. She does not want to lose her job and salary and is quietly passive and submissive, hoping he might stop. He doesn't. They have sex right there on the office floor. A couple of weeks later, he does the same thing but she refuses this time and threatens to report him—until he reminds her that she allowed him one time before and that they were mutually consenting adults. She realizes her threat is shallow and that a conviction would never stick. He forces her once again and rapes her at work. Who can she tell? Who would believe her instead of him? There is no physical evidence and she feels trapped forever.

The neighbor next door did such a major favor for Mr. and Mrs. Greene by replacing the roof on their house. He refused to accept any payment and now Mr. Green thinks the world of him. But Mrs. Green thinks differently! One night when her husband was working late, their next-door neighbor came over to borrow a cup of sugar. He raped her instead. She never thought that he could do something like that and that it would happen in her own suburban home. As he left, he told her that if she told, he would say she seduced him and offered sex to be the overdue payment for the roof. They both know that her husband really likes and feels indebted to this man and that they would hate to have to move away.

A woman in her twenties decides to break up with her fiancée. She invites him over to break the news and he is furious. She insists he leaves and as he walks to the door, he grabs her and says "one last time, let's do it one last time together." She tries to fight him off but he pulls her over to the bed, rapes her, and leaves.

Acquaintance or date rape is especially devastating because you lose your ability to trust in people. Your trust of the opposite sex is demolished and ruined. That is tough. Imagine being worried and fearful around people you know and trust. You wonder if you're a good judge of people and now think you're not. After all, we're taught in life to avoid strangers and not friends. This is life changing.

MYTHS: The word "rape" conjures up dark images of a masked man with a weapon that surprises an unsuspecting woman, throws her to the ground, and sexually assaults her in a secret dark place where her screams are never heard. Yes, that does happen, but only about one-fifth of the time. In about eighty percent of all rapes in the USA, the woman knows the man. Half of all USA rapes occur within one mile of, or within, their home. Other types of rape occur when an employer, acquaintance, or date—someone she knows, and who has no weapon—overpowers her. Rape can happen just about anywhere and to any woman. It's more commonplace than we think. More women suffer from this than we think.

Many myths abound about why some women do or don't get raped. Some believe that nice women don't get raped—yet "nice" has nothing to do with rape. Another myth is that only attractive women are raped—yet "beauty" has nothing to do with rape. Another is that a girl should be too smart to allow that to happen—yet "intelligence" has nothing to do with rape. Another is that if a woman did not fight or scream that she was not really raped—yet "strength" has nothing to do with rape. Freezing up is a common reaction to being raped—remember that. Some say that women secretly desire to be raped—yet no one enjoys being brutalized and humiliated, fearing for her life. Some think that if she is not hysterical afterward, then she wasn't raped—yet she is just happy to be alive.

The most ignorant but most prevalent belief is that some women deserve to be raped because of what they're wearing, where they're walking, what they're doing, or who they're dating.

People believe that the woman does or did something wrong to cause this crime. Yet when a person is robbed or murdered, do we blame them? Do we blame the convenience-store clerk for being robbed? Was it his fault that he was there at the wrong time? Was it his fault he did not stop the armed gunman? If you had your car stolen, was it really your fault that someone stole your car? Let's stop blaming the wrong person and start getting angry at the right person.

All of these myths and theories only inflict further humiliation upon an already hurt and damaged woman. The last thing she needs to hear are your unintentional accusations and questions beginning with the word "why." That isn't a wise word. *We create these excuses to feel safe in this world.* We think that rape happens to bad girls, prettier ladies, younger women, or to very sexually active women. This makes us feel more secure when we are not belonging in those categories. Women like to think they could never be raped because they're much smarter, older, and wiser. They think that they dress more modestly to ever be raped. They feel they have a husband who would protect them. They believe they could talk the man out of it, or simply that they would never allow that to happen. *Not only do we end up with a false sense of security, but we also end up with a self-righteous spirit.* We think that we're far too careful, smart, intelligent, persuasive, or strong to ever get raped. We end up losing our compassion for criminal victims.

MOTIVES: Men who rape women want to dominate and humiliate the woman. They want to overpower her and assert some kind of chauvinistic sick control over a woman. These are angry men who want to control someone else, and they use sex as their weapon of choice. It is a crime of violence more than of passion. They seek sexual and personal superiority by taking advantage of women they view as helpless. Men who feel inadequate, frustrated, and angry are the ones who will express their rage by raping a woman. After a rape, they feel more powerful and finally in control of something. It's a matter of power and not persuasion.

Men who rape come from all backgrounds and are both young and old. You cannot pick them out in a lineup or crowd. They are all colors, shapes, and sizes. They usually know their victim and blame her for his actions, if ever found out. Most plan the rape ahead of time and rarely use weapons. They believe that men have a right to control and have sexual access to women. They usually view pornography of some sort. They are sometimes married and have an available sex partner. Lust is *not* always their motive. Like other sinners, they are simply selfish people and unconcerned about the consequences of their own actions or about the feelings of others. They know what they want and are determined to get what they want. *It's a sin issue more than a sex issue.* And that is why church leaders who know the Word of God are the key people who are best equipped to deal with selfish people who sexually rape others.

Violence against women is never appropriate.

A woman never deserves to be raped. A man never has a right or a reason to rape a woman, ever. Understood? He is responsible before God for what he does and cannot blame someone else for what he decides to do (James 1:14). He *can* and *must* control himself regardless of the amount of temptation, even if it be sexual temptation. She can be naked in front of you and teasing you but you still have no reason or right to ever rape her!

God describes a rape in detail in 2 Samuel 13 with Amnon's rape of Tamar. Amnon felt frustrated since it seemed impossible for him to do anything with her. He grabbed and forced her and refused to listen to her. Since he was stronger than her, he raped her, and then hated her with an even more intense hatred. Anger, lust, and a thirst for power is what motivated him. How did she feel as a result? She felt disgraced, knowing that a wicked thing was done to her. She is left alone in a state of shock and mourning, weeps aloud, and then lives out her life as a desolate woman. Read this story over and over to see what happened.

You see the sinful desire to dominate and possess—under the guise of love or law or lust—in King David's taking of Bathsheba in 2 Samuel 11. He raped her!

Anger, lust, and power are described in Shechem's rape of Dinah in Genesis 34. He wanted her as his wife and was selfish to the point that he ordered that she be brought to him. Then, he violated her and treated her like a prostitute in doing a disgraceful thing. His was an act of violence and deception which in turn caused a reciprocal act of violence. Those who found out about the rape were filled with grief and fury.

Grief and fury accompany rape—so do not discourage the woman or anyone from expressing this emotion at first. Don't label this anger as sinful and wrongful. Instead, help them to grieve that something wonderful has now been taken away. Do we tell those who mourn the death of a loved one to immediately quench and stop their sorrow or anger? In rape, there is a definite death of dignity, trust, security, confidence, and innocence. Let them grieve; let them vent.

Alcohol is sometimes a contributing factor in rape.

In half of all rapes in the USA either the victim, the perpetrator, or both had been drinking. It lessens the restraints of the male and the awareness of the female, increasing the probability of rape. In 2 Samuel 11, David encourages Uriah to get drunk since he knew that Uriah was thus more likely to go home and have sex with Bathsheba. When Bathsheba later announced her pregnancy, Uriah would not suspect David as the true father. Also, read Genesis 19:31–36 to see how alcohol and sexual attack are linked. Do you remember the little-known story in Esther 1 where King Xerxes was drinking too much and commanded Queen Vashti to be brought before the crowd for display? Alcohol makes sexually selfish people worse. (Pastors, have you ever mentioned this is your sermons about alcohol abuse? What a golden opportunity you now have! Now, you have some new insights.)

Sometimes it is mixed drinks, and sometimes it's mixed signals. The man and woman are on totally different levels and planets. She wears a dress she considers flattering but he considers seductive. He spends money on her which makes him think he deserves more than a goodnight kiss. When she gives that kiss, he takes it as her sign to go further. She says "no" but he thinks it means "try harder." She's been taught to be submissive, and he takes it as her being *per*missive. She remains silent, and he takes this as a message that she enjoys it. She does not. She quietly and simply freezes up, as a legitimate response. After it's all over, he blames her for allowing what went on and she blames him.

The church must be much more careful in teaching the concept of "women's submission," since men will take advantage of passive women and violate them.

MINISTRY: Rape causes rage, panic attacks, worthlessness, shame, fear, disorganization, confusion, turmoil, anger, depression, false guilt, self-blame, social withdrawal, and loss of confidence in a woman's abilities to make decisions or have control over her life. Her world has been turned upside down. Now is the time to minister wisely and choose the right words and actions as her helper.

Every church leader and Christ-follower needs to be a rape-crisis counselor. Just because someone does not come personally to you does not mean it is not all around you. It already is. Maybe one reason they don't confide in you is that you don't convey the sensitivity and warmth they need to feel in order to share this with you.

They are also ashamed of what has happened to them. That might be why your church ladies don't tell you. She feels dirty and was stripped not only of her clothes but her self-trust and self-dignity. As one woman told me, "What they did to me is not even done to dogs." Would you want to have to tell that story over and over?

Sometimes women don't label it as a rape, and try to deny it. That's what we all do sometimes in order to cope with a hugely traumatic and life-changing event. If you asked them if they were forced against their will, they will answer "yes," but if you ask them if they were raped, they sometimes answer "no." The answer depends on the question—so be wise in choosing these right words.

False guilt is another reason women rarely report rape. They feel that they somehow provoked or deserved it. They usually blame themselves—saying they should *not* have worn that outfit, walked alone in the parking lot, accepted that date, or taken that job. The list goes on. False guilt is a hard feeling to simply erase but we have the wonderful verse of 1 John 3:19–20 to share with rape victims. God is greater than their accusing and condemning heart—much greater. By blaming themselves, they talk themselves into thinking that if they do this or that the next time, then it won't happen again. That's the way we think in life.

Fear is another reason for silence. Many rapists leave their calling card behind with the words "If you tell anyone, I'll come back and kill you next time." Fear of death is not the only fear she has. She is also afraid she will not be believed, that she will be blamed, that she will be rejected by the loved ones she needs most, or that she will lose the ones who hear her story, retaliate, and get arrested.

So she suffers in silence.

There are so many reasons she doesn't share it. Here are some results:

She's angry—at herself, at men, at the mall security, at her husband or family, at the media for portrayal of women, at the police and courts, at the man who raped her, and at the uncaring God who allowed such a horrible thing to happen to such a holy person who simply tries to be a good Christian in life.

She's scared—of going out at night, parking lots, going on a date, being alone, being touched by her husband, of having contracted AIDS, of smelling a similar cologne as her rapist, of seeing her rapist again unexpectedly, of being so close to death, and of her parents or husband who might kill him and she then loses them, too.

She's confused—about why it happened, whether it could have been avoided, whether her date really did like her, whether she encouraged him somehow, about who to trust now, about sex on her honeymoon night being pleasant when it was so disgusting and painful during the rape, about why she felt somewhat physically aroused with the sexual contact of a rapist, about why it is taking so long to heal, why she seems to look much older after the rape, why she gets panic attacks, why she fights more with her husband now, why she hates all men and resents all types of leadership (that includes you, pastor), why she's much more drawn to women now and has changed her sexual orientation.

She's withdrawn—since she feels so dirty, soiled, used, useless, defiled, degraded, humiliated, and ugly now. She thinks everyone knows about the rape and is looking at her. She wants to stay home but doesn't like to be home alone. She thought others cared but now wonders. She feels trapped, since her loved ones won't let her go anywhere and are now unintentionally turning her into an emotional cripple who is totally dependent on them. It's so very easy to do.

It is the soothing gospel of Jesus Christ that will heal the woman who is raped, and it is the same liberating gospel that can make the rapist change and repent.

The following examples are sermon suggestions, actual words, and counseling tips that can be used as you minister to rape victims and offenders:

THE LIFE OF JOB: Job 3–31

Job had friends, like we do, who believe that a person gets what they deserve in life. That is true many times, but not all times in life. Sometimes you get much more than you deserve, as we can see in God giving us His only begotten Son and that while we were yet sinners, Christ died for us. Sometimes you get much less than you deserve. Something terrible happens and you did not deserve it—and it was *not* your fault. We all tend to fall into the false thinking that it might be our fault if something bad happens to us, that we caused it. Much of life *is* cause and effect, but not all of life. Job had friends who tried to supposedly comfort him with these same thoughts but they were rebuked by God.

People do the same thing when it comes to rape. We think the same way that Job's friends did—that you got what you deserved or caused—and we tell the woman who was raped that somehow she was at fault too. "You should have done this instead of that"; "You should not have dressed that way"; "You should not have been there by yourself"; "You should not have dated him"; or "You must have done something to encourage him or cause this." We try to comfort, like Job's three friends, but end up condemning women instead. We accuse; we blame the victim and not the victimizer. It's easy to say that, but we are dead wrong at times.

Maybe you've been thinking that about your own experience without realizing it. You actually started believing that it *was* your fault. You blame yourself. You became your own worst enemy and now, like Job, you need to hear God speak *His* words to you and ignore some of your well-meaning friends or your own thoughts. We just don't know why some things happen as they do but God alone knows—as He tells Job in Job 40:8–14 and 41:11.

Job rightfully claimed his innocence in this book; what happened to him was *not* his fault. Rape was not your fault either. You did not cause or deserve it. God tells us the reason for rape: "each person is tempted when they are dragged away by their own evil desire and enticed" (James 1:14). Put blame where blame is due.

Please give your confusion and hurt to God. He can heal you from your rape, since He heals the broken-hearted. That is what happened to Job. He survived and recovered even though he never found out "why" his children, possessions, and health were all taken away. Your trust, dignity, sanity, confidence, peace, and joy were all taken away, along with a lot of other things. I understand. God does too.

One thing that was not taken away was Job's trust and faith in God. Yes, he struggled with his ups and downs, as you will. But he also overcame evil with good (Rom. 12:21) and Job is the one who said "Though he slay me, yet will I hope in him" (Job 13:15). That won't happen overnight but it can happen with you. Bringing your pain to God, just like Job did, is the only way to recover from rape.

LEVITE AND HIS CONCUBINE: *Judges 19*

There are young men and older men in America with the exact same attitude toward women that we read about here in Judges 19. They think that girls and women are objects of pleasure or wrath for men to use as they wish. Might you be one of them? Oh, you would never come out and say it but you think it. This sin is serious and does even more serious damage to others and yourself. Pornography makes a man think like this—it makes a boy or man have a terribly poor view toward women who happen to also be made in the image of God. Male chauvinism is not new; it's thousands of years old as we see in this text: "Do to them whatever you wish" (Jdgs. 19:24). That is rape!

That is the cause of rape, and we also see the effects in this story. The woman is devastated. She is exhausted, ruined, dazed, motionless, humiliated, and left for dead. God understands how a woman feels after she's been sexually used and abused by a man. He described how she felt and how you also feel. He describes another woman who was raped in 2 Samuel 13. She was desolate, weeping, a woman whose life was changed by one man who also believed that women can be used to satisfy himself. If you are one of these men, you need to repent. You need a complete overhaul of your mind and life and that can begin today by receiving Jesus Christ as your Savior and Lord. And for those boys or men who have already done this, you need a new power to change how you think, what you watch, and how you treat women. You need a Savior. If you're one of these women, you need to recover and restore what was lost. God will help you to do that. Ask Him.

JOSEPH AND POTIPHAR'S WIFE: Genesis 39

Joseph did his very best to remain sexually pure but instead was blamed wrongfully for what happened. He was innocent but was treated as the guilty one. He was the one put in prison while the one who wronged him remained free. Potiphar's wife was the one who should have suffered, not Joseph. She's the one who seduced, attacked, and then lied about the whole episode. Just imagine how Joseph felt while he sat in prison—treated as the criminal when he really was the victim here. Easily, he could have been consumed with anger, rage, bitterness, confusion, and cried out for justice to be served. All these emotions you might have felt, too.

Girls and women who have been raped experience these same emotions. They sit at home in their own physical or mental prisons while the criminal is still free. They're consumed with fear, worry, panic, hatred, grief, bitterness, and revenge. They feel like Joseph might have felt, and experience the same emotions as he did.

God got Joseph out of prison though, just like He can get you out of our own prison and set you free. Rape victims don't have to stay in prison; God opens the door and wants to help you walk out with His help. He did that for Joseph and wants to do that with you. God had *big* plans for Joseph, and has big plans for you. The rest of the book of Genesis shows us those plans; but He first had to get Joseph out of his prison. The same is true of you; are you willing to be set free?

JUDAS: Mark 14:43–47; Matthew 26:47–49

Judas was one of the select few who had the privilege of being closer to Jesus. As one of those twelve first disciples, they did lots of things together. They were all friends, pledging loyalty to each other and to Jesus especially. They trusted each other. In fact, when Jesus announced that one of them would ultimately betray him, not one instantly pointed his finger at Judas. No one suspected him, did they?

Judas was an excellent actor. He acted as one who loved Jesus but in the end, he betrayed Jesus. He took advantage of his close relationship with Jesus and then used Him for his own personal gain. You know the rest of the sad story.

There are many people just like Judas walking around today, more than two thousand years later. There are people who betray a trust, don't keep their word—people who act like they like you but then use you and hurt you. Something they said or did baffles you because you thought they were your friend. In the neighborhood, at school, at the office, in the family, in the church—it can be anywhere. You trusted them, you thought they cared for you, but now you're disgusted at what they said or did to you. You have a Judas in your life; if not yet, you will have a Judas one day.

Acquaintance, office, or date rape is an example. A lot of young men act like Judas on a date. They act so lovingly and trustworthy—maybe even a kiss on the cheek, just like Judas did with Jesus—but they have a hidden agenda and an ulterior motive. They want more than a kiss on the cheek at the end of the night and overpower her. Are you a Judas who did this? Do you feel guilty like he did?

Have you taken advantage of someone like this? Have you hurt her deeply? You pretended to be so very nice but when you didn't get your way, you got more selfish and forced yourself on her. You forced her against her will to do something. Like Judas, you betrayed a trust and you now need to apologize and repent of this.

Or might you be the one who had a Judas do something like this to you? Even though Jesus was not surprised about his Judas, you were shocked at the behavior of your Judas! Jesus knows that. He knows how you feel and why you're hurt, mad, bitter, confused, and that you don't know who you can trust anymore. Jesus understands; He had a Judas in His life, too. After the kiss on the cheek He was brutally beaten, spit upon, stripped of His clothes, and humiliated by others. He truly knows the feeling of being betrayed by someone who only pretended to care, and He also knows how it feels to be left all alone after being victimized.

SAUL'S TREATMENT OF DAVID: 1 Samuel 23–26; Psalm 56

David was innocent of any wrongdoing to Saul. Nevertheless, Saul wanted David dead, and his one consuming goal in life was to kill him. Saul is obsessed with that and pursues, threatens, humiliates, and has David fearing for his life. To make matters even worse and harder to understand—at one point and earlier in their relationship, Saul liked David and was nice to him.

Maybe you are just like Saul today, or maybe you identify more with David. Maybe you've gone on a rampage like Saul and went as far as raping and violating a girl or woman that you know and even, once liked. Maybe it was a total stranger. You were obsessed like Saul—maybe with her beauty or innocence or friendship—and you went after her, like Saul went after David. You hate to admit it but you identify with Saul. You were out of control, yet someone else suffered for it.

Or maybe you feel like David here since you have had your own Saul hurt you? It could have been a total stranger, a friend, or a casual acquaintance at work. But he did something to you. He pursued you, threatened you, intimidated you, humiliated you, and tried to attack you—like Saul did to David. Maybe he went further and sexually assaulted and raped you.

Like David, you feared for your life right then. Many psalms he wrote during his life were about people trying to hunt and hurt him and how he felt as a result.

His peace and your peace were taken away, your body was violated, your dignity destroyed, and your sanity was suspended. It was all taken away from you in the twinkling of an eye. And now, it's hard for you to sleep knowing of your own personal Saul who pursued, tricked, forced, or sexually assaulted you.

David was a hunted man who also felt helpless. Much of his life, he also had evil men who were his enemies lurking after him, and he felt helpless. He gave that helpless feeling to God and found his *only* hope in trusting God to take care of Him—before, during, or after any attack on him. God does that for us.

THE GOOD SAMARITAN: *Luke 10:25–37*

Here is one story that you hear once and never forget it. Most people who don't even like the Bible remember this famous story that Jesus told here. Which person catches your attention the most? With whom do you identify the most? Which person is your most favorite and least favorite in this story? Some people here actually identify with the person in verse 30: someone who just happened to be in the wrong place at the wrong time and as a result of that, they were robbed, stripped of their clothes, and left for dead. It can be called a rape.

Has that happened to you? Maybe not all but part of this happened to you? Did you just happen to be in the wrong place at the wrong time? You were caught off guard and robbed? Maybe you were stripped of your clothes instead? Maybe you were beat up and left for dead, or thought you were going to die right there?

And then, people who were supposed to care for you did not know how to respond and just walked away, like in our story. They walked away and ignored the whole thing by not believing you or blaming you. Notice that Jesus didn't blame the person who was robbed or say he should not have been on that road to Jericho all alone. Jesus did not accuse or blame the victim here at all—but we do.

We are told to weep with those who weep in Romans 12:15— not walk away. We're not supposed to blame them for being victimized, robbed, or raped. We should not interrogate, accuse, or analyze them. We're supposed to listen and let them tell their story, whether it be robbery or rape. We should sympathize.

We're supposed to show mercy, according to verse 37—even when we don't know what to say or do for the one who was victimized by someone else unfairly and sexually. Show mercy. That person *is* your neighbor and we're told to love our neighbors.

Do you feel like the man who was stripped of his clothes and left for dead? Did someone do this to you? Did others hear your story and walk away in a sense? Are you mad now as a result of both injustices done to you? Jesus is the friend you need who would not have walked away. He spent His whole life *not* walking away but walking toward people who felt helpless, robbed, and raped by others. He is the one person to whom you can give this pain and panic. He told this story.

THE SADNESS OF BATHSHEBA: 2 Samuel 11

Has anyone ever wondered how Bathsheba must have felt in this story? We like to condemn David for what he did and understandably so. He took something and someone that was not his. He overstepped his boundaries. The list could go on and we all know this famous Bible story pretty well. But what about her? We're told it was David's idea and he was responsible. Nowhere in this text is there any hint that *she* is the one who seduced him, wanted this to happen, or consented to this unpleasant or ugly sexual experience. Bathsheba did not sin but was sinned against. Did anyone stop to ask what loss and grief she must have felt? Her whole life was turned upside down by this rape, and that is what it was. David's great sin became Bathsheba's great loss. For no rational or good reason, her life was changed suddenly because of one man. In the matter of a few moments, she was kidnapped from her home by the king's men.

King David wanted her and used her for his own pleasure, his sexual pleasure. And then he wanted Uriah, her husband, to do the same thing after he did. And then her rapist, King David, kills that same husband. And then, the child who was conceived as a result has his life taken away. What is Bathsheba left with?

Bathsheba has a broken heart, a murdered husband, a changed life, and a dead child. What rage she must have felt toward David and rightfully so! What grief and mourning she must have experienced over the death of her husband and then her child! She was in charge of her life and suddenly she is at the mercy of a selfish powerful man whose only concern was himself. That is *so* unfair.

That is so common though, today. So many millions of women today are in the same shoes of Bathsheba and feel like she felt. Are you one of these women? Because of one man, your life is changed and your heart is broken. You also lost so many things near and dear to you—things that should not have been taken from you. You did nothing wrong but you were wronged and used by a boy or man who overpowered you. God knew of what David did and reprimanded him for it. He also knows how you feel and asks you to come to Him with that hurt and loss.

ADDITIONAL AND ADVANCED "RAPE" STUDIES IN THE SCRIPTURES:

THE STORY OF SENNACHERIB AND HEZEKIAH: 2 Chronicles 32; 2 Kings 18–19

Develop sermon/counseling ideas that can relate to rape. Study precisely how Sennacherib taunted, ridiculed, and threatened Hezekiah, who cried out to the Lord for help. (A similar story of Goliath and David in 1 Samuel 17 could be developed.) God rescued him from this offender and gave him comfort.

THE STORY OF HAMAN PLOTTING AGAINST THE JEWS AND MORDECAI: Esther 3–7

Develop similar ideas about a man plotting to do evil against innocent people. Haman was obsessed about harming others who did nothing wrong. Study Mordecai and how he reacted to Haman's rage against him and his people. Notice the turn of events. God triumphed amidst the evil intentions of one man and then, He used it for His own glory. This is a deep truth that could be shared with rape victims.

PURITY OF A BELIEVER: Romans 8:1; Ephesians 1; Colossians 1:27; Titus 3:5

The raped woman who is a believer in Christ needs to be reminded that the purity that Jesus gave to her is never taken away in life by anything or anyone. If Jesus lives in her heart, she is *still* clean, pure, spotless, filled with goodness, white as snow—even though she feels the exact opposite as a result of her rape experience. No matter what was done to her, she must believe what God says about her. Her body is still the temple of the Holy Spirit who still dwells in her (1 Cor. 3:16; 6:19) and He lives there forever (John 14:16). God already washed her once and for all; she does not need to take any more showers to wash away the filth she feels. Nothing can undo the purity which He has given her, not even rape. We need to weep with her while we also remind her of what God has spiritually done for her in Christ to replace the memories of the disgusting things a man has physically done to her. That is our ultimate goal in due time. This is tender surgery.

BLAME-SHIFTING:

Examples include 1 Samuel 15 where Saul blames others for his action, Genesis 3 where Adam blames Eve, and Genesis 32 where Aaron blames the crowd for his sin. Use stories like these with insights on how the man blames the woman for what he did to her. Help her to not wrongfully blame or accuse herself for what happened.

GOD'S OMNISCIENCE OR OMNIPRESENCE:

Rapists think no one knows except for them and their victims. They need to be reminded that God knows everything in the past, present, and future. God can't be fooled and will not be mocked. Though it might have been done in the dark, God is light (1 Tim. 6:16) and saw it all. He promises in Proverbs 28:13 that whoever tries to conceal his sin will not prosper, but that whoever confesses their sin will find mercy. Encourage them to confess.

REVENGE, RAPE, AND TURNING THE OTHER CHEEK:

Be careful when you approach this topic and don't be simplistic and idealistic. Are we told that the revenge described in Shechem's rape in Genesis 34 was completely wrong? Were their feelings unjustified and sinful here? Did God reprimand them? Why do you think God ended this chapter with the legitimate and loving response found in verse 31? Should a woman "turn the other cheek" and supposedly not report her rape? Should she just forgive and forget? What did Jesus do when He was struck on the cheek, in John 18:22–23?

JOSEPH AND POTIPHAR'S WIFE: Genesis 39

Try and put yourself in Joseph's place if he would have been forced to have sex with this woman. Not many, but some men have experienced rape upon threat of death with a weapon by a woman. What would you say to Joseph who wanted so much to be a virgin until marriage, but now he was not? How dirty would he have felt? *What would you say to him to relieve his feelings of shame, anger, embarrassment, and disappointment?*

In verse 9, he said, "How then could I do such a wicked thing and sin against God?" Thus, in a rape event for a Christian, a wicked thing has been done against you. Imagine yourself having a wicked thing done to you and against you. How did you feel? How would you feel if this happened to you? Put yourself in his shoes to feel it. How would you counsel him? Would you tell him to just get over it? I hope not.

8

CHILDHOOD SEXUAL ABUSE AND MOLESTATION

Memories of childhood sexual abuse can torment for an entire lifetime. Sexually exploiting an innocent child at an early tender age will cause a multitude of confusing emotions that can suddenly erupt and express rage, later on in life.

When I suggested to Cathy that she allow Jesus come into her life as her Lord, she quickly became agitated, uneasy, and nervous. Our quiet conversation had suddenly took a turn for the worse. She insisted we change the topic. I assumed that she was trying to run from God and thus, I gently pursued the conversation but she resisted me even more. Why did she become so insistent on avoiding this?

The idea of Jesus *"coming into her heart"* vividly reminded Cathy of her father who would penetrate her when she was little. She couldn't get past this picture.

My conversation with Cathy opened my eyes to how sexually abused people will hear your message in a way that is far different than you ever intended it. Seminary never prepared me to evangelize, counsel, or preach to people who share similar experiences to Cathy. *Here are some of the different ways they will hear our gospel message:*

"Giving God your body as a living sacrifice?" What do you think those words from Romans 12:1 might mean to a victim of sexual abuse? Giving God my body? Does He want it, too? What does He want to do with it? If God is anything like other men, no thanks! If God only knew what disgusting things I had to do with my body, He wouldn't want me anyway. I hate my body now.

"Trusting God?" Yeah, right. Look what happened when I trusted my father! I trusted him when he said it was okay, when he told me he loved me, when he told me that I needed to know about sex. Even though it didn't feel right to do this, I still trusted him because fathers aren't supposed to lie. I won't ever trust again.

And when I told my Mom, I trusted her to put an end to all of it but she didn't. She called me a liar and did nothing. She told me to keep quiet. Look what happens when you trust people, even your own parents. Trust God? No way!

"God wants to use me?" I feel all used up right now but thanks for asking.

"God protecting me?" Cathy asked me why God didn't protect her all those years. It went on and on. No one protected her in the past, not even God

"God using evil for good?" Verses like Genesis 50:20 and Romans 8:28 that bring comfort to Christians can bring confusion to all sexually abused women and men. Her dad said that sexual intercourse would end up being "good for her" too.

However, there was one word that Cathy did understand as we talked that day: *submission.* She definitely heard and knew that word and what it meant. She knew the Bible verse, "Children, obey your parents," that her father quoted hundreds of times. She learned to obey whatever her father said, even though it hurt to have him violate her innocence and pleasure himself. If Cathy ever does become a Christian in the future, you probably won't find her questioning God about things. She's been taught to submit and obey but never to question. By the way, Cathy was living with a man at the time of our last conversation. Trusting a man enough to marry him? That was totally out of the question for her.

Cathy's story is similar to the millions of women who have a tough time celebrating Father's Day. Please remember Cathy as you prepare your sermon for that occasion. You might think this problem doesn't exist in your church. Yes, you have wonderful men and fathers in your congregation but some are not perfect. Please don't think this is limited to females; men suffer the same emotional hurt.

I once conducted a weekend retreat on the topic of "The Fatherhood of God." Without ever intending to, I opened up some serious wounds with a lot of weeping that weekend. I didn't expect the huge avalanche of counseling appointments as a result. There were stories of sexual contact within fine Christian homes from both men and women who were subjected to unwanted touch when younger.

Is this one of the church's biggest secrets today?

It shouldn't be. People view sex lightly and children negatively in our society. People also know that children are not likely to be AIDS carriers. Add these and other factors together and you shouldn't be surprised.

The people who should be least shocked are those who know their Bible. There is nothing new under the sun, remember? There were people in the Old and New Testaments who had incestuous relations (Gen. 19:30–38; Lev. 18:17; 1 Cor. 5; 2 Cor. 2). So, why are we so silent about this? If God is brave enough to include this in His Word, why are we so very silent and scared?

It's been going on for a long time. You have women who wonder why it's taking so long for their husband to change their baby's diapers. You have people who want to kill the person who molested their child, even if it be a relative. *You have women and men who have a hard time showing physical affection to people but especially to their own children (or spouse). They spend too much time trying to protect or please their children now. No one knows that this is why they do this.* You probably have women or men in your church who have secretly carried this burden for many years. Might you be the one who can set the captives free? Might you be the one who gives them the peace of God that passes all understanding? *How many people are the victims of childhood sexual abuse?* No one truly knows that number. One reason is that this is done in private and secret. Offenders know how to get away with it and are masters at manipulating situations of secrecy. The offender also wants to make absolutely sure that the child never tells anyone about it. They know who to choose and how to get away with their crime. There is also no standard methodology or definition that is consistently used by every organization that collects this data in their unique studies or surveys. It is quite safe to estimate that one out of every four girls and one of every six boys under the age of eighteen are sexually abused each year in the USA. However, only about ten percent of all child sexual-abuse events are actually reported. For every single confirmed report, most experts believe there are anywhere from ten to one hundred cases that remain unreported. One in five children are solicited sexually while on the Internet. Females are the victims of sexual abuse in eighty-five percent of the cases, and that's why I will mostly use the feminine pronoun in this chapter. Sexual abuse of males is equally heartbreaking. Boys are equally devastated and even more embarrassed to tell anyone, feeling immeasurable confusion and shame as they grow up into men.

Ninety percent of child sexual-abuse victims know the perpetrator, and seventy percent of sexual-abuse victims are abused by family members—nuclear or extended. It might be from the father, stepfather, mother, mother's boyfriend, uncle, brother, etc. Sometimes, the sexual molestation is initiated by strangers or adults engaged via Internet conversations. The average victimizer is a heterosexual man in his thirties, and the average victim is around ten years old. Seventy percent of child sex offenders have between one and nine victims. A serial molester has about three hundred victims in his lifetime.

Are all children affected in the same way? No, it all depends on the actual circumstances. It depends on how frequent it was, how long it lasted, how painful it was, how the non-offending adult responded to the news, how old the child was, how the child is related to the offender, how they were threatened not to tell, and what type of personality temperament the child has. Another important factor is whether this crime is validated and justice was served or not. There are so many factors.

Researchers estimate that far more than one million children under eighteen are now being talked into some type of sexual contact from a known adult. *Why do preachers talk about the one million children who are aborted each year but again, we say nothing about the one million children who are molested each year? Why are we so silent or selective on which sexual topics we address on Sundays?*

Why have pastors not gotten involved? "Job security" is my honest answer here. It won't make your people happy and sure won't increase your pastoral longevity. It is not something your people want to hear about or think about in church. Oh, they hear it on the news but don't want to be reminded of it in their safe haven. They come to church to find peace and not be reminded of the tragedies of life. And I understand that, I do. People get upset over the very thought of this action.

God's people typically don't know what to do with their confusing emotions of rage and disgust. And then, Christians aren't "supposed" to be angry, remember? They'd rather avoid the issue. We don't know what to do with or say to the man or woman who would do such a thing to a little child. While those feelings are understood, we must not be repulsed by these men in life. How can you truly help them if you hate them? We also don't know how to act toward the abused child. We are scared to be too affectionate or authoritarian with the child. We don't know how to handle the manipulations that the perpetrator will attempt on us. We don't know who to believe, how to detect false accusations of molestation by a spouse who is being revengeful and hateful, who to tell, how to detect it, how to prove anything, and we sure don't know how to help the entire family who now is suffering as a result. We are scared to say the wrong thing. While all these reasons are understandable excuses for noninvolvement, they are still insufficient. I hope this chapter equips you to become more skilled in helping sexually molested children and all their families.

As with rape, we ask the wrong questions by beginning with the word "why." Why did you let this happen? Why didn't you tell anyone? Why didn't you tell someone else who might listen? Why did you let it go on for so long? What did you do to cause your dad to get so mad? Why didn't you scream? Why didn't you run away? Why don't you just forgive and forget now as an adult? The list goes on.

We also have to be careful not to verbally criticize the father or mother in the presence of the child. We must not forget the emotional attachment that a child naturally feels for their father, regardless of the abuse. The child usually feels responsible for the unpleasant aftermath or legal consequences. She'll probably get blamed by someone at some point for something, before it's all over. Yes, this often happens.

REASONS: Some say that those who were sexually abused in their past will surely abuse others in the future. While forty percent will re-offend, not every survivor will re-offend again. While we know that our actions have a futuristic ripple effect upon others, this is just too simplistic of a root cause for this action.

The real reason is the exact same for all the other sexually inappropriate acts that we've looked at in this book: sin.

A sinful nature does not respect or concern itself with anything or anyone but itself. Self is supreme—even at the expense of others. It's all about you. I will do whatever it takes to get what I want. My way is all that matters and I am number one. That is the nature we inherited from Adam and Eve. Sinful people use other people (even God) to satisfy their own selfish desires. *Sexual molestation and abuse is ultimately a spiritual and not a historical problem.* Thus, the pastor should be most equipped to have the solution to sexual abuse and never isolate survivors. The liberating and transforming gospel is the most powerful force to have.

Sinfulness expresses selfishness in two ways as it pertains to incest and abuse. Sexual childhood offenders are usually and extremely *dependent* or *dominant.*

The dependent man has given up trying to cope with life's problems. He feels overwhelmed and has withdrawn from adult responsibilities, adopting a passive role. Social skills or sexual relationships which require negotiation, commitment, and mutual consent are viewed as too difficult. So he selfishly and sexually turns to a child in order to feel fulfilled, successful, and powerful again. It's easier.

In contrast, the dominant man is very rigid, opinionated, outspoken, and unmoved. He doesn't give up (as the dependent man does); rather, he tightens up. He cherishes his role to rule and control others. He feels that people need to be policed and that he is best equipped to do so. This spills over onto children. All sinners enjoy power, independence, and control. That's what we do and want. We will bully people or sweet-talk people into getting what we desire. Sexual abuse, incest, and molestation are deceitful and domineering misuses of power. *Seduction and secrecy are their calling cards.* They study children carefully. They are masters at getting children to do what they want when the time is right, and then get them to remain silent about it for years. They say, "I'm going to teach you a special game that will be our secret"; "This makes me feel good and I'll buy you something nice"; "If you tell, Mommy will be real mad and Daddy will have to leave and it'll be your fault. So be still and be quiet; Daddy will take care of you; Daddy loves you"; "This is what big girls do with big boys and you want to be a big girl one day, right?"; "This is what adults do to each other and we're going to be adults now." Doing something so selfish to a child (and then threatening to hurt her even more if she tells) is one of the most dangerous things they do.

We all have succumbed to the belief that sexual expression is the best method to fulfill physical or emotional desires. Sex is deemed as *the* way to express yourself and whatever you're feeling at the moment. A creature seeks another creature instead of the Creator to fulfill needs, once again. It's what we do.

And as addiction is lurking around the corner for any and every behavior in life, some men become obsessed with children and become pedophiles. These men have intense sexual fantasies and urges involving children. They calculate their moves cleverly to get what they want and work themselves into positions of trust.

How do victims of incest, sexual abuse, or molestation feel as a result?

SELF-BLAME. Children (like adults) happen to be egocentric, believing that the universe revolves around them, right? When there's a death or divorce, the child thinks it's somehow their fault. Children blame themselves. The same is true here, especially with incest or sexual abuse. They don't blame the adult or their dad or mom—so they blame themselves. *Sometimes their false guilt leads to self-deprecating or self-destructive behaviors.* One overweight woman felt so bad inside for all the things she had to do with her dad that she wanted to look outwardly as bad as she felt inwardly. We have the good news of the gospel that we don't need to punish ourselves any longer; that's why Jesus was punished. He was punished for our sin and for the sin of others and we don't have to inflict it upon ourselves.

Sometimes these children grow up into women who feel they're always wrong—or wronged. One pastor shared, "If I don't greet her on Sunday, she wonders what she did wrong and thinks I'm mad at her. I'll get a phone call on Monday. I have to walk on eggshells around her. She doesn't even realize this."

BODY SHAME. They are ashamed of what has happened to them. They feel less feminine now. They carry that around, daily. These victims believe they're damaged goods, forever. They wonder if they'll ever look pretty, have babies, or enjoy sex. They're uncomfortable about dating, being seen in a bathing suit, being seen naked in a locker room or on their honeymoon night, or even going to the gynecologist. They feel so dirty or filthy and sometimes and they can act frigidly.

You would too if that was done to you. You'd feel like damaged goods if you had to endure such painful and perverted sex. You'd view your body very differently if you had a man five times your size thrust himself into you over and over as you just lay there and waited for it all to be over. *I also know women who were afraid of closed elevators or spaces because it reminded them of the feeling of suffocation when their adult offender was on top of them.*

Body sensations can easily trigger memories which cause her or him to freeze up, without being fully aware. A wife didn't tell her husband why she hated sex with him. Oh, she pretended to enjoy it but it made her feel like she was being slowly suffocated to death. He never knew that his wife's uncle was very obese. Just the idea of walking to the bedroom—even though years later—instantly brought back these memories.

Another woman confided to me that she never wore dresses but only would wear oversized sweatshirts, blouses, or pants.

She did not want to look feminine lest any man do to her what her father used to do with her after watching porn.

PROMISCUITY. Some women learned to hold back and hate sex, but some had the opposite reaction. They learned to let loose and give their body to whoever wanted it. They know that their body can be a powerful tool in life and get them some very special gifts. About eighty-five percent of prostitutes were sexually abused when younger. They learned way too much and way too soon about sexual activity.

CONFUSION. Victims of childhood sexual abuse don't know the answers to basic questions we take for granted. They're uncertain about their own identity and role in life or family. Does my dad love me or hate me? Will he protect me or hurt me? Am I a child or am I an adult? Am I his daughter or his wife? Does he do this because he likes me or doesn't like me? Am I supposed to do this or not? Does he do this with mommy? Am I supposed to take care of mommy? Why doesn't she stop this? Doesn't she love me either? Why does this feel bad and sometimes good? How does something this wrong hold my family together? That's why *so* many young girls run away. We think she is rebellious, yet she's trying to escape.

HELPLESSNESS. Your heart breaks as you see the pictures that a sexually abused child will draw to describe either themselves or their victimizers. They see themselves as defenseless and hopeless; many draw themselves with no arms or legs on their body. Or they might draw a large slit near the zipper of the pants and they grow up seeing all men as sex-crazed maniacs. They'll not get married.

These girls don't know how to stop it, how to get away, how to tell their dad to stop it, who to tell, what to tell. They were told they'd be hurt or killed if they talked. She has a dark secret she can't share with anyone and ends up carrying the burden all alone. For a small child, there are not a whole lot of options. Many grow up feeling helpless, unable to cope, and being indecisive. They've been trained to believe that circumstances are beyond their control. They have been told that they can't tell anyone and feel helpless as to how to make the pain go away. *They usually lack self-confidence in the smallest things of life or everyday decisions, as a result.* No wonder that child sexual-abuse victims are three to four times more likely to abuse alcohol or develop drug addictions. They rarely assert themselves; they become passively dependent on other people to make most of their decisions for them. They really do believe others know what's best for them and cling to people who seem so self-assured and decisive. Some will avoid making decisions, and some will go in the opposite direction. They will stubbornly resist and detest any type of authoritarian decision-maker in their life. They become obsessively ambitious and have great careers and wealth instead.

ANGER. Sometimes the anger freezes and launches them into a very deep depression. while other times they'll lash out at the smallest things that remind them of it. Victims of domestic violence also experience these same emotions. Later in life, totally innocent words or behaviors of someone else will suddenly trigger memories of childhood incest or abuse and they can go ballistic.

Remember Cathy at the beginning of our chapter? Whenever she felt like she was being taken advantage of by someone (her employer, friend, supermarket clerk, next-door neighbor, etc.), she would begin to shake and her lips would quiver. Memories of her father who took advantage of her for years were now coming back. And whenever Cathy met someone who seemed fragile, indecisive, or weak, memories of her mother who allowed the abuse would overcome her. Without exception, she would perform her nightly ritual by walking downstairs into her basement and start hitting that punching bag that her psychotherapist told her to purchase. Whenever she felt that rage and wrath welling up deep from within, she'd be sure to make that lonely trip down those steps to her basement.

Forty years later, Cathy is still punching away. That's how our conversation ended, with her going down to the basement. Sometimes though, she told me that she stops punching it, starts crying, and tries to hug him instead. After all, that's all she really wanted from her father. That's all she still wants in life, but her dad now refuses to talk with her and admits no wrong. He tells her it was all her fault that he did this. He passed away without apologizing and she lives in a frozen rage.

How sad that she was given such bad advice in being taught to murder her father in her heart. Wouldn't it have been far better to have told Cathy that one day she could *eventually* forgive her father and pray for him—by the amazing grace of God!

PREACHING TIPS ON CHILDHOOD SEXUAL ABUSE, INCEST, AND MOLESTATION:

This topic will be more difficult to approach than the others we've looked at in this book. Be patient, as you take the time to carefully choose your words in your sermons. Be careful as you try to bring conviction to the offender yet comfort to the victim, all in the same message. *Your job is to make the offender feel bad, not the victim. The victim should not be placed in the same sentence or category as the victimizer.* Complete your thought with one person before you move onto the next one. You want to minister to both but in very different ways. Again, quality is much more important that quantity. Insert a few carefully chosen and wisely worded sentences or paragraphs in your sermon or counseling session.

The following examples are sermon suggestions, actual words, and counseling tips that can be used as you minister to sexual abuse, incest, or molestation victims, as well as to the actual sex offenders and perpetrators:

THE HEADSHIP OF THE MALE: Ephesians 5:23–33; 1 Corinthians 11:3; 1 Timothy 2:11–15

When the Bible teaches that the husband is the head of the wife, it is qualified with the words of "as Christ is the head of the church." Jesus combines authority with affection in His dealings with us, and we are to do likewise. Headship does not mean the woman is inferior to the man. It does not mean the husband is always right but it does mean he is responsible. He's responsible for meeting the needs of his wife and children; he is their pastor. Headship is not to be violent, controlling, or an abuse of one's power. Jesus is our role model when it comes to headship.

Unfortunately, many fathers don't imitate Jesus in the way they lead or love their wives and children. They expect every order they give to be obeyed without question. Some demand that their wife—or child—do things that ought not to be done. It might be illegal, unethical, unscriptural, and it might be immoral. It also might be sexual. They take advantage of their role and also . . . of their children.

As the father-boss, he thinks he can take sexual liberties with his daughter. However, this is a crime! He treats her like a wife instead of a daughter when it comes to being intimate. The father regresses and transgresses at this point. And he knows he has because he'll then make sure his sin is a secret and orders her never to tell anyone about it.

This is wrong. This is not Scriptural headship. Maybe you as a father (or stepfather, coach, counselor, or some other adult authority) have done things like I just mentioned. You blurred the roles of husband and father with your daughter, stepdaughter, or some other girl. You hide behind those verses, even. You need to confess your sin, repent of it, and not twist the Scriptures to your own destruction—or your daughter's. Maybe today is the day you'll come clean.

Many daughters feel defiled, violated, and damaged. Do you have a dad who does these things? Do you have a dad that did those things to you? He forced or made you do things that were wrong. You worried and wondered if dads and daughters are really supposed to do these kinds of adult things. But you were lied to, and you felt helpless before him. You shouldn't blame yourself for what he did to you. And you shouldn't feel ashamed for what he did to you either. Don't let it destroy you. Don't let these memories control your life any longer. You feel like damaged goods, but you are not.

If you're a Christian, you have a new father, a heavenly Father. I know it's tough for you to trust that new Father in heaven because your dad on earth did you wrong. You might not know how to respond to the love of your heavenly Father because your earthly father twisted and tainted "love" for sex and power. God, as your Father, will never ask you to do something wrong. God grieved and still grieves with you. Don't blame Him for your abuse, please. He won't ask you to keep a secret. He won't do something that makes you feel dirty. He won't make you angry. In fact, He makes all things new and does all things well. And He wants you to tell Him about your hurt from the past. He wants you to know how deeply loved and protected you are. He offers you a good future, though you had a bad past.

SERVANTS OF RIGHTEOUSNESS: Matthew 23; 2 Corinthians 11

There will always be hypocrites in the world and yes, even in the church. There will always be people who appear to be so holy, so clean, and so pure—yet they are far from that. They say the right words and do the right things but you don't know all that they do or say in secret. You would never suspect that their life is a lie. They can be two different people. You think you can trust them but you can't. Their outside appearance is far different from their inner heart. Both Jesus and the apostle Paul spoke about these kinds of people in these texts.

You might have a secret or a secret life that no one (but God) knows about. It might include deeply personal, ethical, business, family, or sexual secrets. Jesus knows. He knew about the Pharisees. Paul knew about the false apostles. They all were not what they appeared to be. Paul said they masqueraded as servants of righteousness and angels of light and that's what people think they are.

But they're not.

Churches have people like this today, as they existed in the New Testament times. People are put in or possess positions of authority, trust, and leadership, but they do something that makes you wonder and doubt. Maybe they made you mad by what they did or said. You trusted them because they seemed to be servants of righteousness, but they instead they were servants of perversion.

You're not to blame. Second Corinthians 11:15 tells us they masquerade and have masks. Every October, we wear masks and children especially believe those masks. Children can be easily fooled because they believe the masquerade and mask. Masks trick us and scare us into doing things or believing things.

As a child, you have to trust in order to survive in this adult world of ours. Maybe you trusted someone who happened to have a "mask" on. Someone who appeared to be trustworthy—maybe your dad, stepdad, uncle, relative, brother, babysitter, neighbor, camp counselor, or even a religious leader—turned out to be the opposite. The person who sure looked like a servant of righteousness ended up taking advantage of your trust—and maybe even your body. Sometimes adults pretend to be nice but they're not so nice. Today, grown men and fathers take advantage of their own or other children who happened to trust them. Children are taught to obey authorities at all costs and times, aren't they? You were a child, and children follow adults in life.

Stop blaming yourself. Paul didn't blame or punish the Corinthians who were led astray, in 2 Corinthians 11:3. He knew. God knew. I hope you know, see, and expose those servants of righteousness in your life who weren't righteous at all.

OBEDIENCE TO GOD OVER MAN: Acts 4:1–20; 5:12–42

When you get asked to do something against the will of God, just say no. The early apostles were ordered to be quiet, keep Jesus a secret, and tell no one about Him. They were commanded to not make waves and not say anything. Even though Jesus told them to preach, these authorities told them not to preach. So, who do you choose? These Christians chose Jesus. The authorities tried to intimidate them and hurt them. They ordered them not to speak about Jesus any longer and to keep Him a secret. Especially in our society today, we're silenced.

There are people today who want us to keep Jesus a secret and tell no one. There are also people who want us to keep secrets and tell no one what they did. Like in the text, they are your authorities and surely you'd think they were right. But they are not always right, just like in this text. What they ask is not right and you have to speak up, finally. It's not easy but sometimes, it's necessary.

Adults even ask you to keep things they do, as a secret. Fathers, stepfathers, relatives, babysitters, strangers, coaches—they sometimes tell children to keep secrets. They know that what they do is wrong and demand the child to keep it secret and tell no one. In return for their silence, they promise wonderful things or worse, intimidating threats!

Sounds like our text today, doesn't it?

How hard it must have been for these apostles to disobey people they normally would obey. Their response was simple: We must obey God rather than man. They did not keep quiet.

We should not keep quiet about our Savior. We should not keep quiet about our sexual abuse, about being touched inappropriately, about the bad or sad things we were told to be quiet about when we were children. Some children got tired of keeping it all in and finally told. Maybe their mom (or other family members) didn't believe them and believed the adult instead. That's what happens today. Adults tell children to keep quiet and they have kept it inside for years, telling no one.

Be like the apostles today. Don't keep quiet any longer. Don't allow any man—even if it be an adult or your father or your church leader—to keep their secret any longer. You must obey God rather than man. Come tell me your story this week. Come talk to me, or to a trusted friend or staff member. Tell us what you've done, or what was done to you.

GOD ONLY GIVES GOOD GIFTS: Isaiah 55:1–3; Matthew 7:9–11

God loves to give with no strings attached. He doesn't give in order to get, like we do. He gives because He loves to give. A father usually loves to give to his children. We see Jacob giving Joseph a coat of many colors. Hannah gave Samuel a robe each year. The father gave the prodigal son his ring and a feast upon returning. The Bible is full of fathers who give, but especially God the Father who gave His only Son.

In our text, Jesus knows that parents aren't always perfect. Only He is. Parents happen to be sinners, too, and He calls them "evil" just like all other human beings. Jesus knows the reality that sometimes adults hurt children.

You might be agreeing with me on that. You *know* that your parents are not perfect. You *know* that your mother and father happen to be sinners, like all are. Maybe your father thought he was doing nice things for you and told you that but he was wrong and you knew it. Maybe he convinced himself that he was spending enough time with you but he was wrong. Maybe he was spending too much time with you and didn't allow you the freedom to breathe or grow up as you got older. Maybe he was spending the wrong kind of time with you—bed time with you.

Yes, you wanted his love but not that kind of love. And now you might be thinking that your heavenly Father is like your earthly father. He is not; He only gives good gifts and will never use you for evil purposes. He only gives *good* gifts, re-member? God won't give you a snake when you ask for a fish; maybe your earthly father did. He gave you the wrong thing. He gave you something you never asked for, right? You wanted and only asked for his love, but he instead gave you sex and he made you feel dirty or used. He gave you something you did not ask for, want, or need.

God is very different. God knows exactly what you need in this life. You can trust Him and know that His will for you is good, pleasing, and perfect (Rom. 12:2). Jesus draws the dis-tinction here between an earthly and heavenly father in this text. There *is* a big difference. Jesus is saying you *can* trust God, but not always adults or authorities or even parents. Jesus would not be surprised by incest or sexual abuse or molesta-tion of children, as we know it today. Why are we? Are you like a father who gave his child something very different? Do you need to apologize and set the record straight? Do you see your-self in this text here? Or maybe you have a father who did this to you and gave you something wrong? Now is the day where you can be set free. You can grieve and vent, finally.

THE SINS OF THE FATHERS: *Exodus 34:7; Leviticus 26:39; Numbers 14:18, 33; Jeremiah 32:18*

The Bible shows a universal pattern in which parents exert a huge amount of influence upon their children in both the near and far future. Not only does a man reap what he sows but his children reap what he has sown too. What he does do, and does not do, will have an effect upon his children. Children learn what they see. In the lifestyles of the Old Testament patriarchs, we see how children copied their parents' behaviors in terms of lifestyle, lying, and unfair favoritism. We especially see it in King David and his sons. Children *do* become like their par-ents. What a promise, but what a warning! You do live on after you die—in the memory, or in the lifestyle of your child. This enormous truth draws us to rely on God.

Hopefully, this memory or lifestyle will be a good one that lives on but that isn't always the case. I know of men and women who cry all day on Father's Day because of what their fathers did to them—emotionally, physically, or sexually. The fathers' sins are being visited upon their children. I know of women who have a hard time trusting anyone, even God, or their husband. Why? Their father destroyed that trust and took sexual liberties with them when they were younger. The fathers' sins are being visited upon their children. I know women who have a tough time in having normal sexual relations with their husbands because of what their fathers had done to them. Husbands now innocently suffer because they happen to be married to women who were sexually abused while children. The fathers' sins are being visited upon their children—and even to strangers. I know women who are so unbelievably overprotective of their children now, so that their children won't have to experience what they did as children. The sins of the fathers are being visited upon their children and their children's children. Will the pain ever stop? Will your pain ever stop? This pain will continue to manifest itself in negative habits for a very long time if we don't deal with this pain. Will your sins ever stop ruining the future of harmless innocent people? God's Word is always true and what He predicted would happen, did happen—and you see it. Will you come to Him and ask Him to make the pain from your parents stop? Will you ask Him today to make *you* stop?

EXPOSING AND REBUKING SIN: Luke 17:3; Ephesians 5:11; 1 Timothy 5:20; 2 Timothy 4:2; Titus 2:15; 3:10

It is not an easy task to expose and reveal the sin of other people. Jesus told us in the Gospels to beware of our motives and methods but that when the time finally does come, you must get your strength from God because you're going to need it. Paul told young Timothy that he must be willing to rebuke the sin of those who were older than him and that it was God's will, regardless of the consequences. He was always telling Timothy not to be scared. It's easy to be scared when younger.

I know of one lady who went to her father and did what the Scripture said to do: expose his sin of incest. He exposed himself, among other things, to her while she was just a child. Incest, like any other sin, should be exposed and not hidden away. It must be brought out in the open so people can confess and renounce this sin. Some of God's people don't want to deal with this sin, but how is this one any different? Why should sexual sins be given special treatment and not be exposed or rebuked? We don't get a special dispensation to commit any kind of sin, okay?

My friend went to her father but he denied the whole thing. He said it was her fault, not his. He blamed her instead of himself. It went on for years but it was their secret, as he told his daughter.

We're told in these texts not to keep secret sins in the closet—whether they be ours or someone else's. They should be exposed. Expose and rebuke sin, even if it is from within your own family. That's the command. When people sin against us, we sometimes think that it was our fault and not theirs. That's what this woman's father said to her; that's how she grew up for many years. Instead of blaming her father, she ended up blaming herself for this and now so many other things.

Sooner or later, the time sometimes comes in your life for you to expose and rebuke someone else for their sin and put the blame where blame is rightfully due. It goes not on you but on them. That's what God told Timothy to do and tells us to do. Isn't it about time you lay your burden down? Isn't it about time you owned your own sin? Are you that child or woman— or are you that father in my story?

SATAN'S TRICKS AND LIES: *Genesis 3:4–5; John 8:44*

Satan loves to lie. It's his full-time job and he is called "the father of lies." He will twist the truth, tell you half the truth, or sometimes come right out and tell a total lie to you. His best trick is to make you think that his way is better than God's way. That is what happened here in our Genesis text. He told Eve it would be helpful to her, it would be in her best interests, and that it would do no harm to her or to Adam. He assured her that what she was about to do was perfectly fine.

Satan comes in the form of a shining serpent. Satan never comes in all his ugliness or we would surely run from him. He can speak through a serpent and he can also speak through a person. They tell you something is in your best interests. They persuade you that it will do no harm to you. They tell you they're going to be helpful to you. As adults, we can testify to times we've been duped by our shining serpents at work, in our neighborhoods, in school. We actually believe them.

If adults can be gullible and trusting, how much easier is it for little children to believe everyday lies that are told to them? Children trust more and thus, they can and do get deceived more.

There are some people who know that very fact and take advantage of it. They take advantage of children in a multitude of ways. They are the shining serpents of our society. They make lots of money in movies or television by telling them that alcohol or drugs will solve their problems and make them even happier. And then, there are some adults who promise children that a sexual act would be fun and helpful to them, just like the one they showed in the magazine or video. There are serpents who forced a child into perversion. Might you be one of those serpents today? Might you be one of those strangers or fathers who say or do these things? You know which children are most vulnerable.

You don't look like a serpent. You don't look or sound evil. You promise it won't hurt and that it's in their best interests, just like Satan told Adam and Eve. You tell little boys or girls that this will be good for them and make them feel good inside. You tell your daughter or someone else's daughter it'll make them feel like an adult. The list of lies could go on, and all of them are straight from the pit of hell. Serpent, come forth. Show yourself for what you are and stop telling your lies. Stop being the seed of Satan and ask Jesus to make you a child of God instead.

Or you might be like Eve. You might have easily fallen for the lies of a serpent. Innocent Eve and innocent children have had their eyes opened and they now feel ashamed and hide, like Eve did. How long have you felt ashamed, like Eve did? How long have you been suffering? Your eyes have been opened and you see.

God had the final word with Eve and He had the final word with the serpent.

He took care of her—even after the serpent took advantage of her. Maybe you were tricked, like Eve was, into doing something that changed your life, like hers? Who was your slimy serpent? God can cover your shame as He did with Eve.

JESUS AND CHILDREN: Matthew 18:5–6; 19:14; 21:15; and verses that show His tender attitude and personal ministry to many other children (see Psalm 127)

People in our society have little time or love for children. We're usually too busy to spend quality time with them or answer their questions or go to their games, etc. As adults, we try to keep pace and stay above water. Our children can end up ignored. Our kids just want our presence, not our presents. They just want our attention. That is exactly what Jesus gave them. He treated them like human beings equally made in the image of God. Jesus loves and loved the little children.

Today, there are adults who don't treat children the way that Jesus did. They either don't spend enough time *or* they spend too much time with them—and for the wrong reasons. They'll say it's out of love but it's out of lust. They molest children. Like all sinners we, and they, use people—and yes, even children.

Maybe you are guilty of that behavior and for the very first time in life, you are hearing a sermon about this. Jesus is the One who can help and make you treat children the way that He did—with respect. He can give you a new and nonsexual love for people, which also includes children. But you've got to admit you need help here. "Whoever conceals their sins does not prosper, but the one who confesses and renounces them finds mercy" (Prov. 28:13). Jesus is called "the friend of sinners." He's willing to be your friend as you admit your sin. If others knew of this sin, they would not be willing—but Jesus is offering you His help today.

This same Jesus is also called the Man of Sorrows. He was used and abused; maybe you were, too. He was humiliated and stripped of His clothing; maybe you were, too. Jesus understands the shame and endured opposition from sinful men, just like today's victims of sexual abuse and incest feel shame and have been treated unjustly from sinful men. Jesus knows how dirty you feel, since He became sin for you (2 Cor. 5:21).

Jesus is the voice for children whose bodies have been hurt or abused by others. That includes sexual abuse, incest, and molestation. He comes into those people whose bodies have been used and whose hearts have been broken. Maybe you are one of them. When you were younger, you remember an adult who forced you to do something physical or sexual that you still remember. He lied to you. Maybe he was nice to you so you would be nice to him. There are adults like that in the world who treat children far differently than how Jesus ever did.

Jesus is here to teach adults on how to properly treat children—as children. Jesus also wants children to know that

He is different from all other adults in your life. If you have been a secret victimizer of young children *or* if you've been secretly victimized as a child, Jesus is the One who helps you repent or heal.

FATHERS PROVOKING CHILDREN: Ephesians 6:1–4; Colossians 3:21

Parents, do your children sometimes make you mad? I'm not talking about making you hurt, disappointed, or confused. I'm talking about anger, not hurt.

The Bible also talks about parents or fathers making their children to be angry. The Greek word for "anger" is also used in Romans 10:19 and Ephesians 4:26. God speaks about adults provoking their child or children to the point of absolute outrage. There are lots of ways we adults and fathers can provoke our children to anger. May I suggest the main reason I believe our children get that angry at us?

We don't practice what we preach. We act one way in public and another way in private. No one likes a hypocrite who is far different at home than what others think. Some men have secrets that only their wife—or their children—know about. It could be that both know or only one knows. Maybe only the child knows, maybe only the daughter or stepdaughter knows. She knows what her father does to her and her body. She also knows she's supposed to keep quiet about it and not to tell Mommy or anyone.

There are many men today who have said or done things to their children and have provoked them to anger. Taking verbal shots—or taking sexual liberties—with your child will do that. God understands and gives us help in changing these habits. In Ephesians and Colossians, is He talking directly to you right now?

There are many women today who have been provoked to anger by their dads, just like the Scriptures teach. There are many men today who are equally angry at their moms for their sexual advances made to them when they were younger. They're extremely bitter, confused, and boiling inside. If you are currently one of those children or adults who has been provoked to anger, God understands you. He knows all the ways in which parents can provoke their children to anger. Will you come to Him for healing? Jesus had anger in His life too and can help you deal with yours. He experienced people who terribly sinned against Him but He didn't let that anger become sin. That is not an easy task and you can't do it alone. Wouldn't that be wonderful for you to understand how to do that, like Jesus did?

These messages are going to be challenging to say, I promise you! But God has called you to be a front-line defender of the most vulnerable people on the planet—children. Children should never be sexually wounded and their innocence should never be violated. God has called you to fight evil on the front lines of the battlefield, so I strongly encourage you to use your greatest weapons—the Word of God and the mighty power of God—as you publicly or privately share how God can transform our hurts or habits and make us more like Jesus.

9

PORNOGRAPHY

For many months, I had been trying to help Jim find a wife. Yes, I was playing matchmaker as his pastor. Here he was, a good-looking and godly twenty-four-year-old man who was ready to be married and telling me he was having trouble finding a wife. Jim was discouraged that every relationship seemed to fail and he would end it soon after it began. He was always holding out for someone better for some other reason, and he was beginning to wonder if something was wrong with him.

I wasn't as concerned as he was. I thought he was just being a typical guy. We met often to discuss a variety of topics. You name it and we talked about it. We talked about everything that seemed relevant: being a man of God, dating, relationships, men and women, thought life, God's plan for his life. It was all good. Yet there seemed no progress, no change, and no hope. I was ready to give up until one day—out of the blue—I asked him about his viewing, Internet usage, and reading habits. I specifically asked him about whether pornography was part of his life, but I wasn't ready for the answer he gave me.

He told me that he had been involved in pornography for the last ten years and had seen thousands of pornographic websites, videos, or magazines. He was not embarrassed or apologetic and saw nothing wrong with it. He really didn't. His dad would give them to him when he was finished with them and sometimes they even watched or viewed them together while he was a teenager. Naked women and graphic sex were hourly and daily parts of Jim's life. He was used to these images.

Finally, we got somewhere! We figured out the problem and soon, the solution. I began to show him how this affects how he viewed women in general and how he might never be content with one woman as long as he compared her to the thousands of other women who occupied his mind. I told him he needed to stop. He didn't think to tell me about it since he didn't see any connection or correlation between these past activities and his present attitudes. And I didn't think to ask.

You'll be amazed at how you'll get to the root of a wide variety of personal, emotional, sexual, relationship, or marital issues when you begin to probe and directly ask the person specifically about pornography!

I now ask all the time. I ask boys, girls, teens, college students, men, women, wives, fathers, mothers, etc. I assume that pornography might be hidden away somewhere in their life. It comes to my mind instantly and I ask people gently.

I believe we are standing at the source of the problem, the eye of the hurricane, the epicenter of the earthquake. You must get to the root and reason. Pornography is one of *the* main reasons for today's catastrophic increase in sexual addiction, crimes, and victims. It's also a huge hidden reason for many divorces. You'll read about a rape but not about the pornography found in the rapist's home. You'll hear about a child being kidnapped but not about the high price that many pedophiles will pay to obtain children. You'll read about a child being molested but not about the child pornography later found in the home of that offender. You'll listen to a couple having sexual-intimacy issues but not be aware that one wants the other to view porn in their bedroom in order for the other to sexually release. Our country is quietly raising rapists, creating sex addicts, and breeding child molesters in the secrecy and comfort of our own homes and password-protected computers. Porn is now in your pocket with your cell phone, twenty-four hours a day and seven days a week.

You'll hear about what to do about the adult bookstores but not about what to do or how to counsel and preach to those adults who go into those bookstores. Preachers will tell you to boycott television shows or the companies who sponsor those shows or how to safeguard our computers, but not about how to help those who are sexually addicted to their computers.

They need help and hope. They need to overcome this addiction with God's help and be transformed by the renewing of their minds. *They need to experience spiritual victory over this sexual struggle.* This is intense warfare for their very soul, and thus it is the preacher, pastor, and Christian counselor who should be able to help most.

There are three types of pornography: softcore, hardcore, and child porn. Softcore is found in almost every store that sells books or magazines today. It's everywhere and accessible. It's not only found in your adult bookstore anymore. (Closing down an adult bookstore is a small victory in light of alternative outlets.) It's also easily rented at home or seen online. You don't have to sneak out; you can just push a button and it is served piping hot. Millions of kids, left unattended at home after school, see soft porn daily. Soft porn has become as American as apple pie and is often considered harmless and inevitable today.

Hardcore involves a more violent nature taken toward women who end up raped, urinated or defecated upon, hanged, hurt, tortured, beaten, or worse, etc. Child porn shows nudity of young children or actual sexual activity with adults.

Of all the people in the world that should NEVER be surprised at this intense attraction and addiction to pornography are those who truly do know God's Word. Read Job 31:1; Psalm 101:3–8; 119:37; Proverbs 4:25; 6:24–29; 27:20; Ecclesiastes 1:8; Isaiah 3:16–25; Matthew 5:8,28-30; 6:22–2;

2 Corinthians 4:18; Hebrews 12:2; 2 Peter 2:10–19; and 1 John 2:16–17. Know these if you want to minister to women and men who have been poisoned and overpowered by porn.

Clearly and continually, God states that what you see with your own two eyes will drastically influence how you engage your mind and live your life. One of our greatest assets—or enemies—in life happens to be our eyes. They are rarely ever satisfied and our eyes bring death to our minds, if we are not extremely careful.

Why do preachers rant and rave about something that is so easy to fall into? Clearly we must warn people about porn but also understand people enjoy it. This is not rocket science here. Why do we act surprised and shocked? God sure isn't.

The Bible speaks abundantly about the struggles we will always have with our flesh and lustful passions.

God knows how easy it is to get addicted to porn. He especially describes that struggle we will have as part of the sinful nature we inherited from Adam and Eve, who were originally tempted *by their eyes* and the desire to possess what they saw with their eyes (Rom. 7:5–25; 8:5–14; 1 Cor. 5:9; 6:12–13; Gal. 5:13–19, 24; 6:8; Eph. 4:17–19; 5:3–14; Col. 3:5–7; 1 Thess. 4:5; 2 Tim. 2:22; Titus 2:12–14; 3:3; James 1:13–16; 1 Peter 2:11; 4:2–3; 2 Peter 2:18–19).

Any activity in life is addictive; every activity in life is addictive. God talks often about the subtle, deceitful, enslaving, and progressive natures of any and all sin. And sexual sin happens to be one of those types of sin, so why are we shocked? God has given us numerous stories, people, and lessons in the Bible about how easy it is to give into our fleshy and lustful desires, which includes our eyeballs.

Porn can easily turn into a lifestyle; it is not a childish and harmless habit to indulge. Like with anything, you think you want and need more to achieve that first high. It's so much more than seeing naked women in the privacy of your own home, computer, or cell phone. There are predictable repercussions and inevitable consequences. Yes, boys will be boys but they sometimes turn into men who molest innocent children and rape unsuspecting women. Porn grabs you and gets a hold

on you. Then it escalates so that you want more and more explicit and graphic images to make you satisfied. You become
gradually desensitized to it and what was once unthinkable is
now quite natural to you. Finally, you are so immersed in your
memory and mind that you can't help but imitate and act out
what you see. Internet pornography *is* the most available but
dangerous crack cocaine of the sexually addicted today.
A handful of Bible verses will *not* erase the thousands of
pictures they have already seen.

*Remember that a picture IS worth
a thousand words as you try to help
people who want to be freed of this
addictive habit and lifestyle.*

You'll need to do more intensive surgery and not put a
little bandage on a deep wound.

Here are some related topics you should know about some porn or sex addicts:

PORNOGRAPHY AND CHILD MOLESTATION: There are
many websites and magazines showing children in sexual activity
with adults, other children, or even animals. Where do those children come from? Most are from ages three to eighteen and some
were tricked, seduced, kidnapped, drugged, and photographed
to produce porn. Most child molesters who were discovered and
arrested had child pornography in their possession or home and
admitted to initiating and imitating the sexual behavior they saw
modeled in their materials. They rarely use violence toward their
victims; they instead use pictures of other children performing
sexual acts in order to persuade their victims to do the same.

Pedophiles use porn to soften children's defense against
sexual exploitation. They're shown nude pictures of adults with
each other or with children. Some child-porn manuals have
given instructions on how to lure children from playgrounds,
how to abuse them without leaving marks, how to have sex with
a very young girl, and how to threaten children so they won't tell
their parents. Some sites or magazines have carried advertise-
ments from young men or couples who are rich and will pay any

price for children who are minors. Easily available softcore porn is increasingly showing bolder depictions of younger children in sexual contact with adults in recent years. Public acceptability of supposedly harmless websites or magazines would quickly be questioned if the facts were publicized to the masses.

PORNOGRAPHY AND RAPE: Substantial exposure to all intensities of porn suggests a correlational connection to sexual coercion, violence, or unwanted sexual aggression. Porn shows women who don't mind being forced, with their initial response of "no" really meaning "yes." Rapists (and all of us) act out the behavior they view. States and countries with the highest circulation of porn viewership and readership also have the highest rape rates. Again, these little-known facts are so important but often ignored. People want what they see.

PORNOGRAPHY AND WOMEN: Females are presented as weak and helpless, submissive and sex-craved objects who can't wait to be violated and played with. They are adult toys to tinker with, and dehumanized objects to abuse and discard. (Yes, there is tons of porn out there now for women who want to see naked men.)

Men must be discipled and trained on how to communicate with and not try to conquer women. They must incorporate into their new mind-set the liberating fact that all females are equally created as they are in the image of the Almighty God (Gen. 2:24). This is crucial. Jesus was born of a woman (Gal. 4:4). Women are to be treated with respect as equal heirs of the gift of life (1 Peter 3:7). Women are to be treated with absolute purity (1 Tim. 5:2). Male and female are equally one in Christ without distinction (Gal. 3:28). There is no longer any types of personal superiority or sexual hierarchy when it comes to interacting with women. When a person is in Christ, the old is gone and the new has come (2 Cor. 5:17). With conversion comes a new way of thinking and acting toward women. All the images and portrayals of women in porn must be swept away and replaced with biblical images, godly portrayals, and strong role models. They need a major overhaul in their minds. Preachers, can you do this?

Church is the best place to start this revolutionary restoring and re-training of men addicted to porn, and I suggest some practical tips. These converted men must be wisely placed (with subtle supervision) with godly men and couples in a variety of spiritual church events. These men should be matched up with a husband-wife team in local evangelism, community ministry, support groups, home Bible studies, etc. They need to see that women are spiritual creatures—not just physical ones. They need to see eternal and not temporary realities. They need to be slowly and purposefully taken off their life-support system of fleshly, dirty, and sensual thoughts and transformed into a new realm. Men addicted to porn need to read or listen to books authored by Christian women and see materials showing Christian women doing God's work effectively. This will be a slow but key process.

PORNOGRAPHY AND SEX: In porn today, sex exists without love. It is raw sex and ritualistic intercourse. It is not a spiritual union but a physical using. There is no tenderness or gentleness. There are no consequences and surely no children. There's no giving, only getting. How you perform and how you are pleased are all that matters. Orgasm is the ultimate goal. The emphasis is on endowment.

Along the way, natural and normal sexual relations with your spouse becomes just plain boring. The videos and websites are much more creative or outrageous. The types of sexual positions that can be achieved are much more ingenious and numerous. Sexual intercourse becomes more bizarre and painful to the woman.

A man wants to do new sexual things that are definitely not pleasurable, natural, or easy for any woman. He begins to think that women really do want it that way and sex becomes rough, forceful, mechanical, sadistic, and selfish. Sexual positions, partners, and practices are definitely *not* mutually agreed upon by the husband and wife, as Scripture teaches they should be. These men have sex with a centerfold and website, not with their wives. Sometimes they need to literally bring that magazine or show that video with their partner in order to be satisfied. No matter how humiliating or painful it is to his wife, his orgasm is all that matters. Wives desperately want to end this marriage they never imagined.

I have counseled women whose husbands are deeply immersed into porn, and I hear their heartaches as they always think they are second-best now. You have no idea how horrible they feel. They have been told that something is wrong with them since they aren't able or willing to do what he wants to do and what he saw on the Internet, in the movies, or in magazines. She's told she is frigid and cold in bed and that she's not woman enough at times. There are millions of women and wives devastated by their mate's pornography, and these ladies truly believe that they're flawed, abnormal, odd, and inferior. They desperately need grace and healing also. Once again, the best person to help them is their pastor. Can you?

PORNOGRAPHY AND MARRIAGE: Since the wife or girl-friend can't produce or perform like the other hundreds or thousands of women he has seen, the man feels entitled and compelled to go elsewhere. Sexual desire takes precedence over marital vows once porn has become commonplace in a marriage. Adultery is common for porn addicts in the quest for the ultimate sex partner. The wife can't produce the goods he wants and he goes on the prowl for delivery. Her body is not as curvy or flexible, her breasts are not as large, her taste for sexual adventure is not as wild, and her mouth is not as willing. The list is innumerable. Soon after he has exhausted all the possible sexual positions, he then goes after different sexual partners. A spouse enslaved to porn is never content, never satisfied. He is just not as enthusiastic about the wife of his youth anymore and no longer do her breasts alone satisfy him (Prov. 5:19). He instead plunges into a world of fantasy, not reality. He feels much safer in a world of pages, pictures, partners, videos, websites, passwords, perversions, and sexual positions. The last thing the porn addict wants is a spiritual partnership. He is hooked and soon helpless.

The following examples are sermon suggestions, actual words, and counseling tips that can be used as you minister to couples, women, and men who have been affected by porn in a multitude of surprising ways:

THE STORY OF ACHAN: Joshua 6:17–19 and chapter 7, especially verses 21–25

No one would have suspected Achan of privately sinning against the Lord. He was a member of the congregation of Israel, a fine upstanding citizen, and excellent soldier. No one suspected him of this type of sin; his name was not the first one mentioned as the person who probably sinned. He just blended right in.

But God singled him out; God knew what Achan did and also what he hid. It was something he was not supposed to have and that's why he hid it. Maybe his family knew but we're not told for sure. Achan had a secret he thought no one knew about, but he was wrong. God knew. God always knows our secrets.

Achan got caught. And when he did, he confessed with the simplest of words here: I saw, I wanted, I took, and I hid. These same words and his same story can be repeated every day in church. I'm talking about pornography, magazines, movies, videos, bookstores, pictures, computers, Internet, passwords, websites, chat lines, sex talk. You get the drift.

Many men today are much like Achan, caught up in the same kind of story. They see and they want something—or someone—that they cannot or should not have. But it doesn't end there. Then, they think they must have it and take her.

Some want it so badly that they take and force, rape, or molest—in order to have what they saw or see on the computer, in the movie, or in the magazine. What Achan saw was not enough; he felt he had to take and hide it. Men, you know where you've hidden yours. Like Achan, you think no one knows but God does. God knows everything about you, even your secret places, downloads, thumb drives, and browsing history.

Achan's whole family was affected. See verse 25. Maybe you don't see what your habit has done to them or to yourself. But your wife probably knows. She pays the price by being told how inferior or inadequate she is and that's not fair. You're not interested in normal marital sex because of what or who you see.

It was too late for Achan. But it's not too late for you. Come clean now; confess your secret before your world comes crashing in as it did with Achan. What a horrible ending to the story and family here. Wives and women: if you know that your man is hiding something like this, go speak with him first and if he doesn't listen, come tell me or another church leader. Don't allow your whole house to suffer later on. You've suffered enough.

THE STORY OF KING HEROD: Matthew 14:6–12; Mark 6:21–29

Herod had a weakness and it was women. We know he had a woman who did not belong to him because John the Baptist reminded him. But one woman wasn't enough.

Herod has a party and of course, women are there. This time there is one woman who becomes the life of the party. Her name is Salome.

She dances, but the Greek word here implies a sensual and suggestive dancing. Herod lusts for his dancing centerfold here and says he'll give anything in return.

King Herod turns into a little boy. What he sees, he wants. He'll give away anything to get it—or her. He is hooked and now he becomes a slave instead of a king. He'll do whatever she wants as long as he can look and lust. He gives away someone's life as a result and was willing to give away half of his kingdom. This is a picture of a person who becomes a slave to his passions and to porn.

There are many men just like King Herod. Women are dancing in their heads and beautiful bodies remain in their memories from magazines, movies, or sites. They, like Herod, get enslaved to a lifestyle of looking and lusting and they will give away anything to look: money, time, wives, innocence, or marriage.

A lot of innocent people get hurt, too. They pay dearly for the sins of their fathers and for the private viewing habits of their King Herod. John the Baptist was punished unfairly here and today, others suffer. Women, wives, children, younger boys and girls, whoever and whatever it takes to feed their fantasies. How many John the Baptists have we hurt in America today as a result of pornography? Maybe you've been secretly hurt or victimized because of a man's lust. You identify with John the Baptist in this text and I hurt for you too. Come talk to me or our staff who can help you.

Maybe you identify with King Herod here. You know you've gone too far and made promises or done things you wish you could take back too, like King Herod. You still have time; it's not too late for you to give it all up and ask Jesus to give you the self-control you used to have. He can change you and your struggle with pornography.

THE REPENTANCE OF NEW BELIEVERS AT EPHESEUS: Acts 19:17–20

What a wonderful day that must have been at Ephesus, as the community there watched the public burning of books and scrolls. What a relief it must have been to be rid of these books that had caused so much headache and heartaches before. These people really were converted. They became new creatures in Christ. They began to obey His commands and change their lifestyles. They didn't keep their books and scrolls stashed away at home; they knew they had to destroy all of them. If they kept them, they would have been tempted to return to them. So they burned their bridges behind them by burning these books. What a pleasing aroma that went up to heaven that day. God was pleased and honored.

The same needs to happen today. Some of our books need to be burned. How so? Some of your magazines, videos, DVDs, passwords, and movies need to be burned. You know which ones: the ones that don't fit or help with your walk with the Lord. The Ephesians believers knew this; do you? Are you willing to destroy the things that are destroying you? Are you willing to admit and confess these?

You might think of all the money you'll waste if you did that. The text here says that the value of these scrolls and books was about 50,000 drachmas. A drachma was a silver coin worth about a day's wages. Get your calculator out, as I did, and you get 137 *years* of money that was burned as a love offering for the Lord. I don't know how much money you've spent on your adult websites or print materials but it doesn't matter, since your walk with the Lord is worth much more.

You also need to burn them from your mind and memory. That won't happen overnight, just like these believers didn't forget their years of having their books. But you have to make a start, and God will honor that act of obedience. See verse 20 where the fire of the Holy Spirit descended down when the fire from these evil books ascended up. Isn't that what you really want today? Isn't that what you really need to do today? Let's make that promise to God right now.

THE STORY OF SAMSON: *Judges 14–16*

Samson had roving eyes; he loved to look. His eyes finally rested on a woman who would be his undoing in due time. Delilah—we associate that name today with beauty and treachery. Men who have roving eyes will often find their own Delilah and often, have the same result.

Delilah was out to trap Samson. She used her body and then her brains. It worked. Samson was captivated by Delilah. Day by day, he slowly lost all self-control and finally lost his strength. Only when it was too late does he realize that he could not set himself free. What an amazing story we don't forget.

Many men today are just like Samson. Their roving eyes are not satisfied and they love to look. The name of their centerfold may not be Delilah but it might as well be. Like Samson, they have slowly lost their self-control and strength to fight temptation. Websites, magazines and movies are not enough; they must have more. Like Samson, they're in bondage and can't set themselves free from the lifestyle of lust that now laughs at them, just like the Philistines did to Samson.

But God didn't give up on Samson. The story wasn't over when his strength was. God rescued him and did a mighty work in and through him, didn't He? Jesus Christ wants to rescue you and give you back a brand new kind of inner strength. God can deliver you from the power that binds you, no matter how long you've been in chains. Pornography does not have to have the final say in your life. God has given us this example of Samson to give you a warning yet also hope.

THE STORY OF MOABITE WOMEN SEDUCING MEN: *Numbers 25*

In this story, we see men of Israel engaging in sexual immorality with pagan Moabite women. The women invited the men and they went hook, line, and sinker. Instead of remaining with their wives, they went after other women here. In fact, one man brought a woman to his family and into his own home. His name was Zimri and her name was Cozbi.

I see this story happening thousands of years later with men in our churches. They are bringing women into their homes. Pagan women seduce them too and now these men of God are bringing them into their own home and hiding them wherever a magazine, DVD, video, or website might fit. They try to hide them deep inside their computer so no one can find them. They bring them into their home through the computer, TV, cable, or DVD. And like the family who ended up seeing the adultery of their dad in Numbers, the children happen to stumble upon these pictures and see their own Cozbis that Dad brought home. Men do that today; they bring in Moabite women and also the curse of God. They forget that these women who appear on their screens are Moabites, pagans, and enemies as verse 18 says. Have you hidden those women in your home? What do you watch on TV late at night? God knows about the website women and magazine models in your life. Are you so infatuated by them that you bow down and worship the goddess of lust they represent? Who is your Cozbi? Is your name Zimri, today? Might we see ourselves in this story?

You need to instead be a Phinehas in our story. He was not seduced or tricked by those women. He stood strong. He was mad instead and did something about all of it. He didn't sit around complaining, like most Christians do about porn. How can you be like Phinehas? Start at home first. Clean out your house first, get rid of the magazines or movies and cancel that cable channel showing Moabite women. Get filters that don't allow you to see what you ought not to see. Be accountable. Maybe you need to go and tell your husband, father, or friend about the dangers of bringing those women into his house. God approved of what Phinehas did and He'll also approve of your courage. Get help for your son, boyfriend, father, husband, or for yourself—for whoever is ruining his life through porn.

CONTENTMENT, COVETING, COMPARING: *Genesis 3:1–13; Exodus 20:17; 1 Corinthians 7:2–4; 1 Timothy 6:6*

Each of us has inherited the nature of Adam and Eve and we believe that what we don't have is better than what we do have, just like in the Garden of Eden. We have the desire to want what does not belong to us. We want things and we also want people who don't belong to us.

Women want men they can't have; men want women they can't have. Each man should have his own wife and spouses fulfill their marital duty to one another. But a man will see a woman, sometimes in person and sometimes in a picture, page, website, video, or DVD. He wants her more than he wants his wife. Ouch! All of a sudden, he is not content like he used to be. He compares his wife's body to her body now. Whenever you compare, someone wins or loses. Usually, it's your spouse who loses. She's not as curvy as the website woman he looks at, or he's not as muscular as the man in the picture. Her smile and size, his skin or size . . . the list goes on. It's so easy to compare and lose your contentment.

Through no fault of your own, you've now taken second place and that's not fair. But it is commonplace today in America. The husband or wife breaks not only the seventh but the tenth commandment and you're not as content as you were.

Some women have begun to believe the lies their husbands are telling them. For years, she's been told that it's her fault and that she's not sexy, pretty, or woman enough for him. She thinks she is to blame for her husband's accusations.

Women, it is *not* your fault. Don't allow your man to blame you for how he feels and what he does. Don't let the blame game make you feel inadequate. Get your self-dignity from what God says, not from what any man says about you.

KEEPING THE MARRIAGE BED PURE: Hebrews 13:4

The first thing that comes to our minds about this text is that God would prefer that you be a virgin on your wedding night. He wants the husband and wife together to experience this wonderful gift He gave us, together and for the very first time with each other. That's what we're told—to keep the marriage bed undefiled.

This text doesn't refer only to premarital sex, though; it applies to porn, too. The Lord doesn't want you to enter the marriage bed with previous experiences, partners, or memories. Yes, even memories. It's not right to enter the marriage bed with pictures of other men's or women's bodies in your mind. Entering the marriage with previous *pictures* can do as much harm as entering the marriage bed with previous *partners*. Porn is hurting marriages as the most silent killer.

Those adult websites, magazines, or movies leave their mark on your memory. Be content with seeing your wife or husband naked. Keep your marriage bed pure. Having the memories of dozens, hundreds, or thousands of other bodies will equally defile your marriage bed. You can become impure by what you've seen as well as what you've done before that wedding day. You have lost that innocence. You don't have to have sexual expertise and knowledge on your wedding night. That goes directly against what the world, school, television, and teachers are telling you. Porn defiles your marriage bed. God is more interested in your innocence than your performance on your wedding day or night. Are you?

Here are other Bible texts, topics, and stories to apply toward porn:

The Book of Ruth. Men involved in pornography should read how Boaz treats Ruth with respect and honor. He protects and cherishes her. He sees godly qualities in her and she sees substance in him. Make a list of his acts of kindness he shows. Men involved in porn need to imitate Boaz in their relationships with women now. They need to relate to women based on their inner and not outer beauty. They will need to learn how to treat their wives the exact same way.

Idolatry. Often in Scripture, people are tempted to worship the creature instead of the Creator, which is what pornography does in its essence. See Exodus 20:26 and Romans 1 and all the biblical injunctions against idolatry and use this.

Money. Use the story of Joseph being sold into slavery for profit in Genesis 27 with analogies to those who enslave men and profit from producing pornography. Include 1 Timothy 6:9–10 and Matthew 6:2, 5.

The Life of King Solomon. This is an excellent example for people addicted to pornography and casual sex. Though his life began with great wisdom (1 Kings 3), it evolved into materialism (1 Kings 7; 10) and degenerated into a lustful attraction for women (1 Kings 11). Men involved in porn need to study his life carefully, since many will identify closely with his example. Solomon wrote a lot about the woman's ability to tempt a man in Proverbs 2:16–19; 4:23–25; 5:1–14; 6:23–35; 7:1–27; 9:13–18. Compare these verses to what he says in Ecclesiastes 7:26 and Proverbs 5:15–23 at the end of his life, and the lessons he learned the hard way.

10

SAME–SEX ATTRACTION AND HOMOSEXUALITY

When I began preaching about this very difficult and delicate topic of same-sex attraction, I was not prepared for the death threats I received anonymously in the mail. Seminary class never taught me to call the local police station as part of my sermon preparation and follow-up ministry! My church attendance plummeted to an all-time low as well. I definitely had my talks with the Lord on this experience. I was equally not prepared for the hateful responses I heard from many within the church. It seems they had a special disgust that was stored up for the homosexual, and now they had their chance to finally express their opinion. Others had a special tender spot in their heart from having friends or family who claim to be gay and are proud of it. They still think it's perfectly okay with God and they thought I was out of touch and cruel. Rarely will you find any topic today that is more divisive and explosive than this one. That's why you've probably avoided it, true?

I've listened to all the debate, with some saying homosexuality is a gift from God while others are saying it's a curse from Satan. Talk about entering a minefield. If you want to divide a congregation, this is the topic. If you want to try and unite a congregation, this is the topic. Which category does your church fit in? You might be surprised. I will give you helpful hints I've learned through the years when it comes to delicate preaching and wise counseling on this most difficult topic today.

But first, may I share my long list of *pet peeves* that I've compiled as I've watched the stones being thrown from both sides of the fence? Again, our goal is biblical balance and precedence when it comes to preaching about sexual topics, even this one particular most controversial topic which generates so much discussion and division. Follow me here. . . .

Why are some churches so vehemently vocal about same-sex attraction, yet so selectively silent about other types of sexual sins that run rampant in our society? Why is this one particular sexual behavior treated worse than all the rest of them? On Sunday mornings, how many men who are guilty of date rape the night before now sit smugly in their seats while their behavior is not ever mentioned from the pulpit? Why are women who won't engage in sexual relations with their husband never discussed, but women who engage in their same-sex lifestyles regularly discussed? Why are adulterers ignored while gays are deplored? Why are men wanting other women they see in porn so rarely addressed in sermons, compared to the men who are wanting men who are so often discussed in some churches today? I just picture all of our heterosexual sinners praying, "Lord, I thank you that I am not like these sinners!" (Luke 18:9–14). Why do we rant and rave about the one-night stands of the homosexual, but not of the heterosexual? Why do we speak about the abundance of sexual partners for the homosexual but not the heterosexual? Why do we single out homosexual activity so much more than extramarital or premarital sexual activity? There just seems to be inconsistency.

Why do some preachers speak as if homosexuality was found on every page of the Bible when it is only specifically found in eight different texts (Gen. 19:1–11; Lev. 18:22; 20:13; Jdgs. 19:22–25; Rom. 1:25–27; 1 Cor. 6:9–11; 1 Tim. 1:9–10; Jude 7)? If it is so rarely mentioned in the Bible, then why is it so often mentioned in our sermons? That's a very fair question. Some preachers almost always include this particular sexual sin while mentioning their list of worldly sins. Jesus didn't do that—so why do we? As you look through the Gospels, is homosexuality in His list of sins? He preached more about the misuse of our money than He did about the misuse of our body. Why do we do the opposite? I'm just trying to help us preach and live the way that Jesus did. And yes, I know that Jesus affirmed the heterosexual union of a man and a woman to be the only type of marriage approved by God, based on Adam and Eve (Matt. 19:1–6).

Why does the church not see the fields that are ripe unto harvest within the LGBT community? Even though they portray their economic, social, and marital worlds as brighter than ever before with new governmental laws being added and enacted every new day, many of their personal worlds *are* falling apart with much higher rates of suicide. There is an openness and responsiveness to the gospel here that is rarely seen in other groups. We must respond, not react, to this group as we would to others.

Why will most churches feed the hungry child or house the pregnant teenager but do nothing for the lonely homosexual who temporarily needs a place to stay, so he or she can stay away from temptation? How utterly rare that a church would do simple acts of generosity and charity for the homosexual while they will do it for others in need in the local community. It's usually not mentioned in the church bulletin, is it? Watch and see what happens if you ask church folks to do this one. This is not the kind of Christian hospitality that the church is used to—yet.

Why do some of us seem to blame the homosexual or lesbian lifestyle for almost every other sin in society today? They always end up with this one. Why? What a simplistic view! Doesn't the Bible instead teach that Satan is the culprit? In the minds of some preachers and organizations, homosexuals are the one group directly responsible for the moral breakdown of the entire family and society. Doesn't the Bible instead teach that the love of money (not homosexuality) is a root of all kinds of evil? Why does the church act as if those with same-sex attraction are our ultimate enemies? Doesn't the Bible teach that our enemy is *not* (homosexual or heterosexual) flesh and blood, in Ephesians 6:12? Does the Bible teach us to target this one sin or terrify this community of people more than any other? Why do we alienate when our goal is to permeate—with the gospel?

Why do Christians seem to portray all homosexuals as molesters or militant? This is not true. Let's accurately remember that sexual abuse and molestation are crimes being carried out far more today by heterosexuals than by homosexuals.

Why do pastors spout off a hateful handful of verses from Leviticus or Romans to homosexuals who finally got enough nerve to come to them for help? Is that all you have to say to them? Is that all you know about this? Sadly so. . . .

Why do some churches promote hatred of homosexuality while other churches promote acceptance of homosexuality? Usually, it's one extreme or the other. There has been an enormous cultural shift in society and churches on this issue. Again, my goal is to present truth and grace; we must have both biblical elements. And of course, everyone claims to be much more Christian than the others. We look like the contradictory and confusing Corinthian church, which had totally opposite ways of dealing with sexual sin. In 1 Corinthians 5, we first see them with an open-minded, tolerant, and permissive attitude toward any and all sexual sin—much like today. In 2 Corinthians 2:5–11, we then see that same church adopting a strict, unforgiving, and judgmental attitude toward that same man—much like today. The church around the world has a love/hate relationship for the LGBT community—it's one or the other, with nothing in the middle. Which best describes your church or attitude? Let's be honest here—which are you?

Why do some churches loosen or open up their pastoral church ordination requirements or church membership rolls to practicing homosexuals who have no inclination to change? Do we do that exact same thing for those who practice other types of premarital or extramarital sexual activities? Why the difference here? Why do we give them a special dispensation to sin when we don't give it to others? I don't like it when some say that the true test of orthodoxy for a Christian or for a church is their acceptance of homosexuality or not. Where does the Bible teach this test of orthodoxy? When we are angrily told that "homophobia" is a sin, where does the Bible teach that? Where is that verse?

*How **unbelievable*** is the exegetical disasters and somersaults that some people perform on the Scriptures to justify homosexuality! I've debated, read, and heard them all and they just don't impress. You just can't get around the indisputable fact that the Bible does call homosexuality a sin, an abomination, unnatural, wickedness, and something that dishonors the body and God Himself. He did not make a mistake and He did not stutter. We must align to His teachings.

*How **unbiblical*** when some claim you can be a practicing homosexual and Christian during your entire lifetime, without contradiction. Does the Bible teach this? Can a person be a "Christian thief" during life? Of course not! Yet, 1 Corinthians 6:9–11 lists homosexuality and theft in the exact same list. Can you be a "Christian murderer"? Of course not! Yet 1 Timothy 1:9–10 lumps together homosexuality and murder in the same sentence. Theft, homosexuality, and murder are all sins lumped together from your past, not present. God saves us from our sin, not in our sin. Again, no one is given special permission in this life.

*How **confused*** when some claim that human love is the ultimate test for sexual behavior! Some claim there is no sex ethic but only a love ethic in the Bible. However, God's law (not human love) is the decisive and determining factor of what constitutes any and all distinctive Christian behavior (John 14:15; 1 John 2:3–6). If homosexuality can be justified in the name of love, so can adultery, rape, abortion, and incest. We have to be consistent, not selective.

*How **shocking*** that some writers claim that the Bible condemns homosexual lust while endorsing homosexual love!

They erroneously state that monogamous and tender homosexual love and marriage is given the exact same green light
in the Scriptures as heterosexuals are given. Their arguments
sound convincing at first until you see that God used the most
general Greek word *arsenokoites* in His biblical condemnation.
This basic word used by God covers *any and all* types of ho-
mosexual/lesbian practices—regardless of one claiming to have
lust or love, regardless of their motives or methods. That is really important in our discussion. In Romans 1, God could have
used other specific terms such as *paiderastes* (lover of boys),
paidophthoros (corrupter of boys), or *arrenomanes* (mad after
males), but God uses the most generalized word to communicate His command.

How selective that some are now saying that God condemns
only their actions but not their lusts. We're told that as long
as you don't act upon those temptations that there is no sin
involved and that you can (and must) live the rest of your
life with this homosexual struggle in your heart. Really?
Didn't Jesus already tell us that our adulterous desires are
equally similar to our adulterous acts in Matthew 5:27–30?
Neither homosexual nor heterosexual lustful desires are acceptable by Jesus' standards. *Are homosexuals given special
permission to lust, while heterosexuals are not? Why?* Romans 1:27 says that both the desire and the deed are wrong.
Do we tell a rapist that he can secretly desire to rape as
long as he doesn't actually do it? Do we tell a father he can
secretly desire to have sex with his daughter as long as he
doesn't actually do it? Of course not! Let's apply the same
line of biblical and consistent reasoning to those with same-
sex attraction and not ever put this in a unique sexual category, all by itself. Deal?

How flawed that some teach that the homosexual who has
been converted to Christ must still continue to be a lifelong
slave to his or her homosexual desires, struggles, and orientation. How heretical for some to make such statements. Must
they burn with this painful and perpetual passion for the rest
of their earthly life? The answer for "burning with passion"
is the same for the homosexual as it is for the heterosexual in
1 Corinthians 7:9—self-control or marriage.

Why do we treat sexual temptation as if it were different and harder for the homosexual than it is for the heterosexual?

The Scriptures don't teach this and neither should we. Some have gone so far as to say that this retention of homosexual desire without the ability to fulfill it is "the cross they must bear" as they "experience the sufferings of Christ" with this sexual orientation as their "thorn in the flesh." These are unbiblical assumptions and not what Jesus or Paul meant with those words.

Do we tell a converted rapist that his desire to rape must never be fulfilled but that it will always be his lifetime cross to bear? Do we tell a converted child molester that he will have to be in bondage to this particular sexual urge for the rest of his Christian life? Of course not! God replaces previous desires with purer desires; He doesn't allow us to cling to our sexual sin of choice, does He? Every Christian must be active, not passive, in their own sanctification process. If the homosexuals at Corinth were changed, why not the homosexuals of today? They did not get a special grace or strength that is not available to us. God has not lost His power to change lives and sexual orientations, regardless of our feelings.

How hopeless when homosexuals claim they are born that way by God or made that way by people. Most claim to be victims of their genes or environment. If that is true, why would God inflict such harsh penalties upon the homosexual in Leviticus 20? *God does not create a person a certain way and then punish him or her for being that way.* There are no "innate" homosexual needs, drives, or dispositions. The Scriptures teach just the opposite in that these are "unnatural." Homosexuals sometimes claim no responsibility for, or control over, their sexual orientation or behavior. Yet what would we say if the pedophile claimed they had no control over their sexual attraction to children? What if one's sexual attraction was toward animals? Why do we permissively allow one sexual preference (homosexuality) and not allow another sexual preference (bestiality)?

It's not good when the LGBT community says, "If you change, you're not really gay—if you're gay, you really can't change." How convenient! They win both ways. The homosexuals in the Corinthian church were changed as a result of their conversion to Christ. God's power can change any sexual or non-sexual habit. It's not healthy when people point to their past as an excuse for their present. Yes, many homosexuals were fondled or molested as children, but many who experienced similar sadness did not become homosexuals. A whole lot of people (including Jesus) surely had imperfect parents but did not become homosexual. I know many who had smothering needy mothers or distant domineering fathers but who now lead happily married heterosexual lives. The homosexual community needs to stop seeing themselves as blameless victims who can't help themselves.

How tricky when the LGBT community has one of the largest and most active political action committees and set of lawmakers in the world. I don't like the way they lobby and manipulate the media into presenting homosexuality as totally gentle and innocent. Our legislators have let themselves be intimidated and bullied by gay activists in the rewording of civil rights, disabilities, hate crime, housing, and domestic partnership legislation. We've come quite a long way since 1961, when every state in the country had laws strictly prohibiting homosexual behavior.

How deceitful that the media is selectively silent in hiding the realities of the gay world in which there is a higher suicide, promiscuity, and alcoholism rate than found in the heterosexual community. I don't like it when people quote the widely disseminated but already wrongly proven Kinsey Report about ten percent of the male population being homosexual. I don't like it when monies are frozen on other medical research in favor of finding a cure for AIDS. I hope a cure is soon found but I also hope that a cure for Alzheimer's, autism, breast cancer, or Down syndrome is equally found. Again, I'm just hoping for that grace *and* truth.

Thanks for your patience as I shared my pet peeves, committed by both the church and the LGBT community. All I'm asking for is the biblical balance that few people in the church or world seem to have when it comes to this touchy topic.

ROOT CAUSES: As with all other sexual practices we've already examined in the book, we must be careful that any attempt to explain a certain behavior does not become an excuse for that same behavior. In our efforts to generalize, we must not rationalize. Shifting blame is one of the easiest things that we do in life. *In my years of sharing the good news of the gospel to the LGBT community, I do believe there are three different reasons why people get involved in the practice and lifestyle of homosexuality or lesbianism:*

Pain, Pleasure, Parents.

Sounds simple? It isn't.

I find four parental patterns that are common threads among homosexuals: Looking for Dad, Running from Dad, Looking for Mom, and Running from Mom. Rarely have I ever met with a male or female interested or involved in the same-sex lifestyle who had excellent, stable, and loving relationships with both parents. (And yes, imperfect heterosexuals have imperfect relationships with their imperfect parents as well). You can't stereotype homosexuals into the category of lust-driven militant maniacs who began this lifestyle with an insatiable lust for same sex activities. *This is just not the case. Here are some true life stories:*

I counseled with Todd whose father died when he was young. He never felt the hug and touch of a man while growing up. He was starving for a father's hug of encouragement or support, yet he had never experienced any private or public displays of affection from any man. One weekend he was shown that physical attention by his uncle, which felt *so* good. Eventually, that emotional attention turned into physical affection and Todd only knew how good it felt to finally be touched and hugged by another man in his life. He never forgot how good it felt; that's how he got started. He equated feelings of pleasure with male affection.

An alcoholic father regularly comes home, beats his small son, and calls him a queer, faggot, and sissy. The son grows up not only believing his father but also making sure that he never grows up to be like his father. He'll get his revenge.

One lesbian I know got started in a similar way. She never received any signs of physical affection from her mom, so she went looking for a mother by meeting other women and hoping they would fill that void she felt. Many homosexual men and women are looking for a father or mother figure. Some seek the acceptance or affection they never received from their fathers or mothers while younger in life.

Sometimes the exact opposite is true. Girls reminded Bob of his mother, who wanted physical and sexual affection from him. His father was never at home and his mother was lonely. Bob hated her advances and his anger toward his mother became generalized to all females. He avoids women completely—lest they also try to manipulate and control him like his mother did.

One young boy had his first sexual experience with a girl when he was only fourteen. His girlfriend laughed at him and wounded his pride. He began to think of himself as not much of a male and vowed he would never be hurt like that again during sex with a member of the opposite sex. Sex with a girl was traumatic to him.

Betty's parents wanted a boy but instead got her. As a result, they gave attention only to her "male" accomplishments and personality characteristics. They affirmed her masculinity but rejected her femininity. She felt like a male and in turn, she went looking for another female to complement and compliment her masculine personality traits just like her parents did.

Sandy watched her father beat up her mother all the time. She vowed she would never let any man do to her what her father did to her mother.

Kim expressed uncertainty about her sexuality. Her boyfriend promised her that he would help her discover whether or not she was truly gay. After her degrading and disgusting sexual time with him, she chose women instead.

Barb's boyfriend left her after the abortion; she won't ever be hurt by men again. Diane was molested by her uncle; Susie was gang-raped in college. Each of these women chose lesbian lifestyles—out of safety, pain, and revenge.

Many choose this type of lifestyle for emotional reasons, not sexual reasons. Yes, it starts off emotionally but gradually evolves into a physical and then a sexual expression. The emotional pleasure initially felt is soon synonymous with and equated to the sexual pleasure now felt. Emotional and sexual have become one flesh and they've not yet separated the two different centers of our pleasure. And by the way—that's what heterosexuals also do! True?

Some choose homosexual sex as a narcotic to kill the pain from being rejected or hurt by the opposite sex. An interpersonal relational problem ends up being coped with by a homosexual lifestyle solution. It is not always the pursuit of pleasure, but sometimes it becomes the answer to pain. Just like the heterosexual tries to suppress his or her knowledge of the Creator and tries to find satisfaction with the creature and not the Creator (Rom. 1), the homosexual does the same thing. Ultimately, this is a spiritual problem and thus requires a spiritual solution.

Same-sex attraction sometimes starts off with an ambivalence about one's own sexuality rather than having an attraction toward members of your same sex.

They don't have a problem with their opposite sex; they have uncertainty about their own sex. They don't identify with, have confidence in, or measure up to the societal or parental standards set for their own sex. They are just not sure.

And sometimes it evolves into a lifestyle that centers on the physical pleasure. A young boy is fondled at an early age by another male and feels physical sensation. He enjoys it and equates it with true pleasure. He then wants more. Since his first sexual pleasure came from a man, he assumes that the best sexual pleasure and all future sexual pleasures should also come from a man. People who enjoy physical stimulation in life sometimes experiment with and get addicted to homosexuality in their lifelong thirst for whatever feels different and/or good.

To many homosexuals (as well as heterosexuals), the body has become an idol to worship. Searching for a body (rather than somebody) that they'll feel close to their own body becomes a lifestyle that indulges in the physical but not the spiritual. Romans 1 and 3 describe how anyone and everyone will do anything and everything in this world except search for God. He is the very last on our list.

Idolatry, identity, insecurity, inadequacy, incompleteness! Precisely similar to the heterosexual—the homosexual is also trying to obtain pleasure, satisfy desires, or soothe pain through a creature, when only the Creator will suffice! Just like the heterosexual, the homosexual will naturally substitute, confuse, and equate shallow sexuality for deep intimacy. Again, it's not a sexual issue but it's spiritual. So, why do we especially single out the homosexual in our sermons when both heterosexuals and homosexuals are just searching for love in all the wrong places? Both are trying to find their comfort in the creature rather than in the Creator. Both lifestyles have the same reason, root, and result explained well in Romans 1.

REAL SOLUTIONS: Homosexual impulses, like any and all other temptations, should be treated like all other behavior patterns and not as a unique challenge. For some reason, we've bought the lie that homosexuality is in a class by itself. Same-sex attraction has somehow been wrongly upgraded and also elevated to an unalterable, permanent, and fixed behavior that must fully express itself the rest of one's life. That is just not true. Like any other sexual temptation or activity in life, it can be modified and overcome. Deliverance from any type of sexual or nonsexual sin is not an overnight success; instead, it's a lifelong process.

Here are ten tips that I've found helpful in helping homosexuals:

1. *They should lose the labels that they've given to themselves over the years.* An aggressive rejection of the homosexual identity is central to their future healing. They must truly believe what God has said about their current and future heterosexuality and not what they think of their past homosexuality. Their feelings of homosexuality must be replaced by the God-given fact of their heterosexuality. In Christ, we are new creatures and the old is gone. Bible books like Colossians, Ephesians, and 1 Corinthians, along with Bible verses that affirm their identity and completeness in Christ (Rom. 6; Gal. 2:20; 5:13–26; 2 Cor. 5:17; Phil. 3), are necessary in restructuring their thinking. Like everyone else, they must be transformed by the renewing of their mind in order to discern God's will (Rom. 12:2).

2. *They must rediscover their sexuality before they redirect their sexuality.* First and 2 Timothy describe the godly male and female qualities we all need. They must resume

the growth of their masculinity or femininity traits that somehow got squelched or sidetracked. They need to feel like a man among men and a woman amidst other women— because they are. Boys should especially be invited to join the company of men, while girls should be often included with other women in the church. God created a woman for a man and He created a man for a woman to complement each other in this life. Male and female, He created us and it was very good (Gen. 1:27–31).

3. *Another necessary change will be for the homosexual to eventually break off many of their former dependent relationships or past sexual relationships.* This is *not* easy for anyone. Your whole life revolved around certain people or activities and now you're supposed to radically leave behind of all of that? Heterosexuals have the exact same command and difficulty here, so we're not asking for anything totally new or different. All of the Gospel accounts of Jesus specifically calling people to Himself and leaving their past behind will help ease this transition. He or she must form brand-new, nonsexual and nondependent friendships and relationships with members of both sexes within the church family. Studying verses like Proverbs 1, 5, and 7; Matthew 5; 1 Corinthians 15:33; 2 Corinthians 6:14; Ephesians 4; and 2 Timothy 2:22 will especially help here. *I also recommend reading the biblical stories where dependent relationships became intimate friendships but they did not turn into sexual unions.* Jonathan and David. Peter's possessiveness of Jesus. John's love for Jesus. Paul's relationship with Timothy. Onesiphorus and Epaphroditus. Elijah and Elisha. We're told not to put our trust in people and become overly dependent upon them (Isa. 2:22; 30:2; 31:1, 36:6; Jer. 17:5; Hosea 5:13; Gal. 6:10). Looking for a creature to do what only the Creator can do surely places unrealistic expectations and impossible frustrations upon one's partner—heterosexual or homosexual. *I also recommend the Book of Ruth.* Memorize the personal sadness in the life of Naomi in Ruth 1 and her initial feelings of self-pity (1:20–22). Notice how Ruth depended upon and wanted to cling to Naomi in 1:14–18. This is a deep friendship. This same-sex loyalty and dependency could have but

did not evolve into a same-sex sexual intimacy and we all need to see this story. It is so easy to cross that line but Ruth and Naomi did not and they need not. The story does not end with these two ladies as lovers, just friends. God provided a man named Boaz for Ruth. Trace the tender courtship in chapters 2–3 and the emphasis on her femininity in 3:3. Examine the male leadership of Boaz in chapters 3–4. These are very important lessons to learn for the man or woman who is struggling with their sexuality and personality. Notice the marriage and sexual union of Ruth and Boaz, not Naomi, in 4:13. God's plan is for a man with a woman, and He wants a woman for a man. Even though there was personal tragedy, weakness, and vulnerability, they did not turn to each other for lifetime support and God provided for them. In fact, God gave Ruth a child who was of the ancestry of Jesus, in Ruth 4:17. What a happy ending to a sad beginning—how very typical of our God!

4. *They need to discover that spiritual manifestations of love take precedence over sexual expressions.* They must see that the church is the place where true acceptance and love are found. They need to see the heterosexual single also struggling with similar loneliness and know that God understands. He or she must see that their goal in life is obedience, not heterosexuality. As obedience comes, so will heterosexuality, even though it seems impossible to achieve or conceive at first. He who began a good work in His people will complete it.

5. *They need to learn to treasure the God-given qualities of the opposite sex.* Like many heterosexual men (but for different reasons), they need to truly appreciate women for their femininity, not their sexuality. And similar to heterosexual men, the homosexual man should view the opposite sex in a complementary mind-set, not in a competitive one. A generalized liking of women should be developed before a love for one woman can blossom.

6. *Homosexuals trying to change should be paired into fellowships with people who will function like surrogate Christian parents in their healing process.* Help restore or

reconcile the homosexual man or woman with one or both of his or her parents, if that need exists. Forgiveness must be practiced here. In your sermons about parenting, remember how some parents provoke their children to anger (Eph. 6:1–4) and eventually to lifestyle choices.

7. *Churches should also have support groups that offer hope and wisdom for parents with homosexual sons or lesbian daughters.* They should be put in touch with other Christian parents who also daily wrestle in prayer with God over the choices of their heterosexual sons or daughters within the church.

8. *They need to learn how to deal with people who disappoint or sin against us.* Matthew 18:15–20; Acts 15:36–41; and Galatians 1:11–14 teach us here. Many homosexuals (and heterosexuals) have adopted wrongful, inadequate, and unbiblical responses to coping with painful, parental, sexual, or personal experiences in their past. Without fully realizing it, we all overreact to and run from the very people we need to confront. An important biblical lesson for all of us is learning how to confront in love and speak truth with enemies. *The life of Jacob* in Genesis 25–35 is a great example I've used in helping homosexuals. By no means was this man a homosexual, but some issues in his life are applicable to a person struggling with this. Jacob was a quiet man staying at home, while Esau became a hunter who preferred the open country. Jacob was favored by his mother while his dad liked Esau much better. Jacob was encouraged by his mom to do something wrong. Jacob needed reconciliation and forgiveness with members of his own family. Jacob was on the run, but God caught up with him and then brought him to Himself.

9. *The homosexual (just like the heterosexual) must learn that one's strength and joy comes from God, not people.* Dependency upon people must be replaced with dependency upon God. Jonathan helped David to find his strength in God, not their relationship (1 Sam. 23:16). Isn't that also our goal in every relationship we have? The Psalms are excellent reading materials. Personal security and inner peace

comes ultimately from the Creator, not the creature. The joy of the Lord is our strength (Neh. 8:10); it is not meant to come primarily from people. Learning to live for the approval of God and not people is crucial. Each of us needs to remember that the intense craving for a member of the opposite (or same) sex should instead be directed into a craving and thirst for God. This is a lesson for every human being to learn.

10. *They must be committed to another community to replace the gay community.* The local church should be the haven and home they need. As the pastor and preacher, it is you who must lead the way to make it happen. Despite all the blemishes and warts we have, God's people are still the finest people on earth who are best equipped to show unconditional love to people.

PREACHING ABOUT SAME-SEX ATTRACTION

Just make sure that you mention homosexuality in the exact same ways that God mentions it in the Bible.

In Leviticus 18–19; Romans 1:21–32; 1 Corinthians 6:9–11; and 1 Timothy 1:9–11, we see that God makes it a point to list homosexuality alongside of other sins—some sexual and some not. *Mention it in the middle, not the beginning or ending, of other sins in your sermons.* God does. I use the phrase "same-sex relationships" or "gender-identity issues" to bring up the topic. I then gradually weave the words of "homosexual or lesbian struggles, orientation, choices, tendencies, or relationships" into my sermons. "Same-sex" is preferred, though.

I now cringe when I think of what I once preached when I was much younger. I summarized everything I knew about this topic into one brief phrase: "God created Adam and Eve, not Adam and Steve." Then, I wrongfully paused as a lot of people laughed at my words. I was proud of myself for getting my point across in so few words. So, I thought I was doing great. I wasn't! How unwise of me! I know I lost a whole lot of potential counseling appointments due to the insensitive words that I used. Who wants to meet privately with you when you have communicated such simplicity and insensitivity to their very deepest struggle *and* even made people actually laugh at them as a result? Be careful in your choice of words.

Don't treat homosexuality as something too little or too much in your sermons.

If you treat it as nothing, you offer no hope for the one who struggles with this sin. If you treat it as supreme, you also offer no hope or healing. Either way, all lose out. Don't make it out to be more—or less—than what God calls this. It is sin, but it is *not* called the unpardonable sin in the Scriptures, so preach accordingly.

As you delicately preach on this difficult topic, remember that talking about packing homosexual people into your church might also mean that you should start packing yourself and get your resume out—because you may be soon kicked out. Even though many will say today how they are intellectually accepting and tolerant of those with same-sex attraction, most of them just don't want them involved or engaged in their church or nursery or youth groups, whether repentant or not. Speaking directly about same-sex attraction in your sermons will cause your members to think that they will soon be coming or that they have already arrived. And let's face it: People equate homosexuality with AIDS. When you bring in one, people are wondering if you have brought in the other. And they will leave. Sad but true. As we also mentioned, many come to church to escape the problems of the world and not be reminded of them. All of a sudden, you're reminding them of the one sin or group of people that some seek to totally avoid in everyday life. Make sure your church leaders (and members) are in complete agreement with your new ministry in attracting, converting, and discipling homosexuals.

Take them on a tour through the Old and New Testaments, paying attention to God's people being asked to convert nearby peoples. The books of Jonah and Acts are excellent preparatory work. The Ninevites were especially taboo to God's people and also to Jonah. Their lifestyles were known and hated by people of Israel. The same is true with the Gentiles in the New Testament. Acts records the many controversies aroused when the Jewish believers began to evangelize and reach the Gentiles.

Jews did not like Gentiles. Their first response was not good, but it evolved into great joy and excitement for the church. I wish that the local church would simply admit that they are similar to Jonah, who would rather die than actually minister to certain types of people he personally found distasteful.

However, don't assume all your church members hate or fear homosexuals. Just the opposite can be equally true. Society has shifted monumentally here. Some identify or struggle with this; many have friends that they would love to invite to church to hear a compassionate and competent preacher who knows their stuff when it comes to such a delicate and difficult topic. Is that you or not? The elderly may have homosexual children or grandchildren that they never told you about. And yes, there are some in your church who have failed marriages because of it. Some have had family suicides because of this. They never told you why.

The following examples are sermon suggestions, actual words, and counseling tips that can be used as you minister to those who identify with or struggle with same-sex attraction, along with their families:

THE EXCUSES OF KING SAUL: 1 Samuel 15

All of us have the selfish tendency to shift blame away from ourselves, don't we? We think it's not our fault but our parent's fault, our gene's fault, the devil's fault, our friend's fault. They told me to do it. Everyone else is doing it. I couldn't help myself. We claim not to be responsible for our own actions and will shift the attention to someone else.

King Saul did that. He blamed someone else, the soldiers. He said they were wrong while he claimed to be innocent. Why could not Saul simply say that he gave into temptation? Why didn't he admit his mistake? Why blame others here?

Why do we do that? "I don't tithe because I don't make enough." "I lost my temper because my wife makes me so mad." "I lost my virginity because he wanted me to prove my love." "I withhold sex from my husband because he doesn't compliment me." "I cheated on my test or taxes because everyone else does." "I yell at my kids because they can't keep quiet." The list could go on.

In our effort to explain, we excuse. When temptation knocks, we open the door but then we blame the wind for blowing it open. When sexual temptation knocks, we do the same thing. We blame the temptation or situation, our partner, our genes, our parents, etc. Whether it be heterosexual or homosexual temptation, we'll shift responsibility elsewhere. My partner doesn't give me the attention I need. My parents didn't show me love. Everyone else does it so why not me? That's the way I was born. That's just the way I am, so deal with it.

That is not the way you were born. We have to look at the instruction manual. God created a female for a male and He also created a man for a woman. He invented sex and He invented two sexes, not one. Male and female, He created them both equal in His eyes and it was *very* good. He did not make a clone or duplicate of Adam. He created Eve to be a helper since it was not good that man (or woman) be alone. He knows your deepest needs inside.

People who claim to prefer their own sex need to live life as God wanted us to. No matter what the reason is, you need to let go of your excuses, much like Saul.

I know you might have been hurt in the past. You might be lashing out at some parent or person without even being aware of it. Someone did not give you the love you wanted, or someone gave you the wrong kind of affection that you needed. It felt good at the time and now you think that's supposed to be the permanent pattern. I know what types of temptations or hurts or pains might have made you to choose this same-sex lifestyle. I also respond wrongly, like you do, to injustice and insensitivity around me that is done to me.

But I must not turn those reasons into rationalizations. I can't hide behind my excuses and shift blame onto others for my choices, like King Saul did. Neither can you. Saul finally admitted in verse 24 that he was wrong. He shared how afraid he was of the crowd. Maybe you're also afraid to be different from your school crowd, office crowd, neighborhood, workers, or class-mates. Do what Saul did. Confess that you need His strength to resist temptation. It might be the temptation to hold a grudge, the temptation to hold and have a man instead of a woman, or the temptation to have someone that does not belong to you. Let's admit and own our personal temptations. Let's not claim to be a victim of circumstances, genes, parents, friends, or life.

THE STORY OF LOT'S WIFE: Genesis 19

When we read of Sodom and Gomorrah, we remember the sins in the cities and God's anger shown. This story is also spoken of again in Deuteronomy, Amos, Isaiah, Jeremiah, Ezekiel, Zephaniah, Lamentations, and even in the last book called Revelation! Peter, Paul, and Jude all mention it, too. Do remember, though, that homosexuality was not the only sin punished here when you read Ezekiel 16:49. The same is true today. Homosexuality is not the only sin that God hates today. There are many others. Heterosexual sin *and* nonsexual sin are equally undesirable to our God.

I'd like to draw your attention to another judgment in this story often forgotten. This person was not involved in homosexuality but was deeply involved in Sodom and Gomorrah. Lot's wife has much to teach us about the need to be obedient. She teaches us what lifestyles we need to leave behind and the need to be cutting off friendships, relationships, or associations that would tempt us to sin.

Lot's wife looked back and became a pillar of salt (verse 26). She was also forewarned in verse 17 but decided to disobey. She regretted leaving the place and all her friends. Maybe she felt inadequate to start a new life all over in a new land. Those are some of the same reasons some people stay deeply involved in the homosexual lifestyle. They feel inadequate to start all over and they would hate to leave their friends behind. They depend too much on people and don't trust God enough to fill that void felt. Like Lot's wife, it's tough to just get up, walk away, and leave Sodom and Gomorrah. You don't want to leave, so you look back and long for those memories. You might have also become a pillar of salt without even realizing it as a result and now, you will miss out on a brand-new start in life.

All throughout the Bible, we're told to flee temptation or leave behind places or people who might tempt us to sin and we're asked to cut off or pluck out our personal and private temptations (see or give examples from Gen. 39:12; Prov. 5; Matt. 5:29–30; 1 Cor. 5:6–11; 10:13; 15:33; 2 Cor. 6:14–18; Eph. 4:22–28; 1 Peter 1:14–16; 2:11; or 2 Peter 2:18–22).

Maybe you've been living in Sodom—or sodomy—for so very long that you just can't imagine life anywhere else. You can't imagine the future without your friends living in Sodom and Gomorrah. You feel inadequate all on your own. God had a future all planned out for Lot, his wife, and their daughters. But Lot's wife never discovered it.

As you struggle with your heterosexual or homosexual temptation, sin, or lifestyle, remember the strong warning of Lot's wife. Scripture does. Make a commitment right now to keep your eyes upon Jesus and not look back on your own Sodom and Gomorrah. Will you leave it behind? Or will you linger behind, look back, be tempted to stay, and be swept away in the destruction? What innocent-looking situations or temptations, places or people do you need to run away from, pluck out, or cut off in your daily decisions in order to become a better Christian?

THE PRODIGAL SON: Luke 15:11–32

We're not told the reasons why the son left home. He wanted to spend his money, sow his wild oats, and be on his own—all by himself. He wanted to see if the grass was greener on the other side. We all do. He ran away from his roots, his family, and from where he was loved.

But his thirst and quest for adventure, pleasure, freedom, and independence ended up quite differently than he ever imagined. We're told that when his money ran out, so did his friends. The Prodigal Son wanted to live life with no boundaries.

This scene is repeated every day in America, isn't it? You probably know of some prodigal sons or daughters who have parents with broken hearts and open doors. We also have prodigal parents, friends, workers, husbands, or wives.

Maybe you were tempted by the exact same things—personal freedom, total independence, sex, friends, money. You were attracted to a certain person so you left behind your wife, husband, kids, or parents—thinking the grass was greener on the other side. Maybe you got involved with the ways of the world and became so immersed in business, money, power, or work that you left behind your first loves. Maybe you've backslid in your walk with the Lord and ran away from Him. You've run from your roots, spent all you had, and realized you're still not happy.

Maybe you've gotten involved in a premarital or extramarital—homosexual or heterosexual—partnership right now in your life. Like the Prodigal Son, you were just curious at first or wanted to find someone who would fill the void and scratch the itch. Maybe instead you're running from some pain or hurt. Maybe you got enticed by all the wildness and craziness of life without rules. It is so easy to do. Maybe you're looking for someone to be a true friend. But when it comes to the final tally, it's found right here in verse 16: No one gave you anything.

Like the Prodigal Son, you went looking for love in all the wrong places. You were fascinated with the forbidden. You had to find out for yourself. However, that person didn't fill the void. They still don't. Maybe they left you? People used you, like they used him. Now you realize you're in a pit and can't get out. You're maybe into a lifestyle that you never dreamed imaginable, just like the Prodigal Son was.

Are you starving now like he was? Are you tired of the same terrible-tasting food? Do you know that God has a feast prepared for you—if only you would come to Him? Whatever your reason is for being a prodigal, come to your senses and run to Him. He wants you to return to your roots or be reconciled to one or both of your parents, similar to our story. The Prodigal Son was living a sexually active life with many different partners. Maybe you've had your fair share of heterosexual or homosexual partners and one-night stands. It was not too late for our main character here; he did not sin so badly that his father refused to take him in.

The same is true with you. Come to your senses and say that you've sinned and when you do, you'll be given a welcome and a feast like you never had before. Isn't it funny because the son thought he could achieve that feast on his own but he got his wildest dreams and partied—only when he went back to his Father God. Isn't that what you want in life? Unlike our fickle fair-weather friends, Jesus sticks closer than a brother and you're invited to return home. Prodigal, come home!

TREATING PEOPLE AS A GOD: Acts 14:8–18; 28:1–6. Use other materials from Leviticus 26:1; Deuteronomy 11:16; 2 Kings 17:7–20; and Isaiah 42:8.

We are tempted to read stories like these and feel they only apply to the first century. Idol worship? Bowing down to people as if they were a god? Remote and irrelevant? Not really.

Today in America, we view people as things to worship, bow down to, and as things for which we serve and sacrifice. People become miniature gods—putting your employer's wishes first and obeying him rather than God when it comes to a choice; being too concerned about your reputation and how you look in front of people; living for your children or spouse rather than living to please God first. We bow down to idols made of flesh. All of us succumb to the approval of others.

We all do that. We will search for a member of the opposite or same sex, thinking they will satisfy our soul. Idol worship. We look for some emotional or sexual encounter, imaginary or real. No one seeks after God, as we're told in Romans 3. We search for anything but God to give us peace. We place supreme emphasis on the flesh, body, skin, physique, closeness, intercourse, and intimacy.

To whom do you bow down right now? Which person? Which emotion? Which idol? Which dream? What sacrifices do you bring to your idol? Do you sacrifice your job, family, spouse, parents, reputation, children, and even your physical health? Are you an idol worshipper? I tell you what the apostles told their audience: Worship God alone, not any human being. Do not allow any male or female, regardless of their authority or position—and regardless of how they look or how they make you feel, regardless of whether they are of the same sex or the opposite sex—to take God's place and priority. He comes first, not people.

THE MIRACLES OF JESUS AND THE POWER OF GOD: 2 Chronicles 20:12; Job 42:2; Jeremiah 32:27; Matthew 19:26; Mark 5:25–34; 9:17–29; Luke 1:37; 13:10–17; John 5:1–15; Acts 3:1–10

In each of these stories, the people felt totally helpless here and they were. Most were afflicted and hopeless with some physical condition from birth and they had their problems for so many years. Some were crippled from birth, or had been sick for anywhere from twelve to thirty-eight long years. Yes, some were truly born that way and could not change that. Many people in our same-sex community and society also feel that they were born that way from birth. They feel helpless and hopeless. They believe that they have no personal choice but that this is a fixed action decided since birth—much like some of the people in our texts here. They feel exactly like the folks in these stories. I want to remind you that Jesus instantly healed them, regardless of their past sickness and sadness. No matter how they were born, it wasn't a permanent reality for them. Jesus heals people who were born a certain way or who felt they were born a certain way, too. The only way they were healed was from Jesus. The same is true of you. He takes you in your situation and He transforms that into a totally different reality for you.

Jesus also was unique in that only He helped people who were involved in sexual sin when no one else would or could (Luke 7:36–50; John 4:1–42).

Not only did we see God's miracles but we see His greatest miracle of all: Jesus brings to life what was dead or seemingly dead. Whoever or whatever seems to be dead can be resurrected. Do you know that also applies to our sexuality? Jesus can resurrect your sexuality as a man or woman, even though it seems totally dead to you. He can bring back to life your heterosexuality as He created you from birth. You might think it never existed or even that it died. That's okay. He can still bring it back to life. Nothing is too difficult for God. Jesus is the One to turn to when you feel helpless and hopeless. Ask Him to heal your body or your soul. God's power is abundantly able to do things that no one else can do—even change your current sexual preference and perceived sexual orientation. Jesus does these miracles, too.

11

SEXLESS MARRIAGE

Rare and refreshing are the couples in which there is an equal sexual energy and enthusiasm in both partners when it comes to engaging each other's bodies. Having equally high (or equally low) sex drives makes marriage more enjoyable. Often, the husband has a much higher sex drive than the wife but that is not always the case today. Sometimes the wife wants more sex than her husband. In most cases, one partner is just not as interested, affectionate, or expressive as the other partner and this causes a whole lot of sexual pain and agony in a marriage. Low or no sexual libido is not a topic that couples can usually or calmly discuss. It might be sexual reluctance, resistance, or refusal—this ache still feels the same.

I am not talking about medical, menopausal, or memories causing this reluctance. I am also not talking about refusing an excessive amount or painful method of sex. I know many couples in which their spousal sexual advances toward them will trigger memories of a deeply painful past event in which they were traumatized. I know that a woman's negative view of her own body will play a huge part in whether she offers it to her husband. We know there are physical reasons for both sexes. Fatigue and forgetfulness are common. Some are just wired with totally different love languages and personality temperaments and they never knew how those would make a difference and division. We know there are unpleasant events for both spouses that inhibit, along with temporary situations that prevent. There are so many hidden hurts that spouses don't know about in each other's sexual history or activity. Things might have been done to them (or by them) that they've never told you since they don't want to lose you. *We are speaking here of purposeful, forgetful, willful, or emotional reasons for sexual resistance. That's what hurts the most—knowing the other person can but they just won't.* You can handle it if you know they're not physically able but it becomes a whole new story when you come to the realization that they are just not willing. Once a month or less is usually the number that qualifies for this hurt—as we speak to sexual frequency in marriage.

There are millions of hurting men and women who are just one step away from believing that death or divorce are the only solutions, since nothing seems to move their spouse to be more sexually affectionate. Healing this hurt is crucial!

While one of them sleeps, the other one does not. They lie awake frustrated and humiliated, wondering why they have been sentenced to a lifetime of martial celibacy. Where does the hurting spouse go? What direction should they take? To whom do we speak about it when our spouse never wants to talk about it to anyone else? You vowed to be with only one person in life and that person doesn't want you. They feel unloved, unwanted, unworthy, unattractive, unnoticed, and unsatisfied. They feel deflated, defeated, disgusted, deprived, distracted, desperate, and disappointed. They feel exasperated and humiliated in all of life. Sexual frequency and frankness is never agreed upon and both parties split apart. This misery is rarely shared with anyone else, and especially not the pastor who has been too timid to ever touch upon or tenderly tackle this topic from the pulpit.

Song of Solomon describes a couple who is interested in sex with each other. As a married couple, they are amazingly accurate in how and where they plan to enjoy each other's bodies and delights. This book in the Bible again dispels all thoughts that God is prudish and old-fashioned. This is mandatory material for helping you to help others with sexual reluctance. Chapters 4 through 7 are filled with picturesque metaphorical language in which we see both of them not embarrassed whatsoever in showing each other how much they sexually desire, arouse, taste, and tease each other—as a male and as a female. Both Solomon and his wife are equally aggressive. She initiates. He initiates. We spoke about this already in our earlier chapter in describing the way in which God describes their masculinity or femininity in veiled language. *They can't get enough of each other—and God ordained all of this romance writing.* Many times one spouse feels this is dirty, because they've been taught that from their parents or from their church. God has opened up a window of fresh air here.

Proverbs 5 is another section of Scripture we must know to help both the husband and the wife to relax and rejuvenate when it comes to sexual relations. God wants the husband to be totally captivated and intoxicated with the body of his wife. *How can this happen if she never shares or offers it to him?* Women who suffer from body image issues need to remember that their body is a gift to be enjoyed. They need to be less conscious of themselves and more conscious of their spouse. God wants the husband to be literally taken prisoner and seduced by her sexual charms and be blown away with her beauty. He created all this. He gives married couples a green light, but some person or some event has changed that to a red light now! Again, God is not timid to talk about the things we are. Proverbs 5 is His wording in that He wants the husband to be satisfied with the breasts of his wife in life—only hers. This places the burden upon both male and female to be obedient.

Why are we so very quick to talk about "sex before marriage" as well as "sex outside of marriage," but we won't discuss the topic of "sex inside of marriage"? Why the inconsistency and selectivity? We talk about "sex without marriage" but not about "marriage without sex." If a spouse comes to you, asking you to intervene to end their spouse's extramarital affair, you will talk to the offender. Yet, if another spouse comes to you, asking you to intervene to end their marital abstinence, you will probably not say anything. Why the difference? We talk about "cheating on our spouse" but not about "cheating our spouse out of the gift of sex." We talk about "abstaining" but not about "withholding." Why are we again so selective, when both are called sins in the Bible? God tell us the dangers of having sex outside of marriage as well as the dangers of not having sex inside of marriage. Sex sets apart this marriage relationship from all others in their life. In 1 Corinthians 7:1–9 God tells both husbands and wives *not to deprive* each other of marital sexual relations. There is not supposed to be a sole or unilateral decision where only one person is the ruler, rejecter, regulator, and refuser of sex. A couple is supposed to mutually agree together to partake and to refrain. It's not up to one person's moods and it's equally not up to one person's needs. "One flesh" happens during sex, after sex, and before sex—all three of these. It is a process, not an act. This is also a command, not a casual conversation piece, from the Lord Himself. It is a duty in marriage just like it is a duty for the husband to love his wife as Christ loves us and for the wife to respect her husband. A married man or woman should be concerned about how to please their spouse, according to 1 Corinthians 7:33. Pleasing your spouse includes pleasing them in every way. Deal? You offer your body as a living sacrifice to God in Romans 12 and you also offer your body as a gift to your spouse in 1 Corinthians 7. Both bring glory to God.

Sex without marriage is not good.
Marriage without sex is not good, either.

God is wise when He restricts sex and also when He encourages sex! A sexless marriage becomes total torture for the person being denied and deprived of the vow from their spouse that they will have and hold them forever. One has stopped initiating because the other one stopped reciprocating sexually. If they don't initiate, nothing will ever happen. If they do initiate, nothing happens. His or her coldness has caused your coldness and you've shut down emotionally and sexually in order to preserve your dignity and your sanity. It's not very pretty. Frustration, humiliation, and temptation are always associated with this issue.

Few people realize that the source of so much sadness in so many marriages is because of one of the spouses is no longer interested or expressing sexual love.

There are so many couples in which one has become a sexual martyr for the kids. God tells us that one of the things at which the earth trembles is an unloved woman who is married (Prov. 30:21–23). The same applies to husbands. "Hope deferred makes the heart sick, but a longing fulfilled is a tree of life" (Prov. 13:12). There are many whose hopes are deferred and dashed to pieces. If the church wants to brag about having a great family ministry, is this topic part of the curriculum as you're helping couples to create truly stronger marriages for Christ?

There are probably a whole lot more miserably married men and women in your church and community than you ever realize. Don't be naïve or neglectful. Don't be fooled by their smiling faces and vibrant testimonies. This is the kind of dirty laundry that is especially hidden from church folks, since we don't discuss it. Behind closed doors are things kept secret. We have God's Word which can help soothe and solve their secret or their problem—if only we would just bring it up.

Here are some emotions that describe the hurt from a marriage without sex:

ROOMMATES AND REFUNDS—That's what their marriage has turned into where they are living in the same place but doing nothing more than just sharing space. They coexist but they don't consummate. They've become roommates instead of soulmates and playmates in life, and now one of them wants a refund. This is not what they waited for or thought they were getting. One wants to take the spouse back and present the receipt of regret. *This is definitely not the same person that he or she married or dated, and they want to trade up or give up because they are fed up.* You feel you got tricked into marrying someone who simply said they like sex or that they used to like sex —but now, has no interest whatsoever in sex. Some waited for ten or more years and put their hormones on hold, as told by their church—and this is what they get in return?

ROLES AND RESPONSIBILITIES—Church leaders need to teach and preach more about becoming one flesh where God describes this in spiritual and sexual ways. This sexual act physically shows what God wants in the merging of married couples. It's not about "doing one"; it's all about "being one." Sex is meant to help that. *Our body is not our own any longer in marriage and it is not ours to withhold now.* This kind of biblical teaching needs to be included in our messages and ministries. Sexual needs are legitimate and not to be taken lightly. Emotions are connected. One of you feels it is your responsibility to selflessly meet the sexual needs/desires of their spouse, while the other one thinks their mate is only selfishly using their body. The perfect storm is being created for couples if both are not on the same page.

RIGHTS AND REWARDS—Some spouses think of sex as a right not to be withheld and some think of it as a reward that is given for good behavior from the spouse. That is something to be examined very carefully with probing questions for each. Far too often, the premarital counseling did not delve into these two opposing mind-sets. Again, 1 Corinthians 7 provides the biblical balanced view. For some, sex has become a reward you give on the condition of best behavior. For others, sex is seen as a right to be given to you regardless of what behavior you showed. *There is a middle ground between chauvinism and feminism: the Bible!* Usually, the husband and wife are on totally opposite planetary systems in this. Marital rights turn into marital fights with both people going in opposite corners, sides of the bed, or into separate bedrooms. And when there is a disagreement, it only means that there will be even more time without any sex. Everyone loses.

RESENTMENT AND REVENGE—One of them said or did (or didn't say or didn't do) something a very long time ago (or earlier in the day) and one spouse uses this against them to punish them. Maybe it's a personality trait one doesn't like in the other which has been discussed with very little improvement. You withhold. She rejected him in the past because she was tired from taking care of the kids. He rejected her because he was more interested in the computer or the television. Ask couples what makes their list and be amazed. *They may say they have no energy which is why they usually say "no" but don't realize that they're exhausted from the energy used in staying mad at their mate all day.* We either get hysterical or historical in terms of finding reasons for sexual refusal. We need to learn to forgive, daily.

REPERCUSSIONS—Household chores and casual conversations have come to a screeching halt and stubborn stalemate because of this bitterness in the bedroom. When their sex life is good, it plays a minor part in their relationship. If their sex life is bad or absent, it becomes a major problem in their marriage relationship! This coldness has now spread to other parts of the house and to their relationship. Spousal sexual deprival leads to depression, confusion, disappointment, and then temptation. God knows how easily it leads to extramarital adulterous temptation in 1 Corinthians 7:1–9. *We gossip about the spouse who had the affair, but did we ever speak to that person about their mate who played a key role by their refusal?* Some wonder if God is punishing them now for their previous promiscuity in life.

ROMANCE—Routine without romance is the new lifestyle. It's gone, dead, none, over. *Who wants to continually kiss their spouse when there is no reciprocating response? Spouses feel like they are kissing a wall.* There are no more hugs, handholding, kissing, cuddling, embracing, touching, or eye contact in the bedroom or other rooms. Special romantic dates and days are met with feeling forsaken and even more fighting now.

REJECTION—You have been shut down and shut out. Your advances for affection were ignored or deplored. Verbally or physically, you were pushed away with little or no explanation. You did your best to be the best spouse possible but it didn't matter in terms of helping your spouse to fulfill their vow to enjoy you.

RESIGNATION—A spouse quits trying, stops asking, gives up and just resigns. Maybe you got some really bad advice that it's really your fault since you're just not loving your spouse enough, so now you try even harder (out of false guilt) and it just doesn't do any good. You've been told to love them differently, be more patient, be more aggressive or submissive, or to let your light shine in silence. The list goes on. It doesn't work. People check out and live a life of quiet despair now.

REPLACEMENTS—Porn or adultery could be the reason for sexual reluctance, and it might also be the result. Something or someone became more important. When talking about marital sexual reluctance, be looking for these.

RECIPROCATING—One spouse needs and wants to know they are desired. It's not very complicated. They feel like they are the only one who is ever attempting any type of sexual intimacy and a light goes off in their heads saying "Danger!" It dawns on them that it all depends upon them, with the other not ever initiating nor even reciprocating. All the oneness is one-sided and that just doesn't work in life.

RESOLVING—Speaking the truth in love—not letting the sun go down on your anger, and not blowing up with unwholesome words—is God's wise way for us to resolve conflict (Eph. 4:25–32). This is especially true with spousal refusal! When that doesn't work, it's good to meet with a spiritually mature couple on this. Church should be designating such couples to help other couples with marriage. Titus 2:4 gives wise counsel about having the older women teach the younger women to love their husbands. There is a lot of wisdom residing in your church. Church leaders and specialized staff should be well versed in this chapter's content, as well in the previous six sexual topics or behaviors. All seven of these sexual topics are must-reading!

REPENTANCE AND REMORSE—When one realizes how much they deeply hurt their spouse, that is when healing begins and new habits emerge. That's the way it is with all types of disagreements and disappointments. It's a matter of understanding how much pain the other one feels from feeling rejected. God is best equipped to help us feel the pain of others, especially when resentful.

RENEWAL AND REVIVAL—This is what was promised at the very beginning and this is what must continue to happen, especially when years of anger are stored. The best way to move forward is to go backward in remembering those vows. When I ask husbands if they would still die for their wives in spite of this refusal, they still say "yes"—which is a revelation for her to hear and who now responds by giving her body more frequently to him. This becomes a real breakthrough in their marriage, with the floodgates now open. The marriage thrives and survives because this one issue has been fixed finally. God ordained lovemaking to be plentiful and playful to keep the marriage strong.

The following examples are sermon suggestions, actual words, and counseling tips that can be used as you minister to those couples, men and women who are affected by marital sexual reluctance or resistance:

COMMUNICATION AND CONSUMMATION:
Ephesians 4:25–32

We're told in the Scriptures that communication is absolutely necessary in all relationships. God tells us how to do that in these verses and it's filled with practical wisdom that relates to how we talk with our friends, family, children, spouses, strangers, neighbors, colleagues, and workers—how to get along in the boardroom or in the bedroom, in the car or in the kitchen—everywhere and with everyone. We're told to speak up—not to clam up (don't let the sun go down on your anger) and not to blow up (don't let unwholesome words come out of your mouth). Don't give up and don't get fed up. Talk it out but don't walk out. This is not easy to achieve; it is very hard work. Spouses who want to live out the marriage testimony in Ephesians 5 have to live out the communication teachings of Ephesians 4; it's not a coincidence they follow each other, back to back. There are so many areas of life where we would be happier if we only applied these verses from Ephesians 4—but I think it especially applies to husbands and wives. So many times, one wants to leave because the other one won't listen. So many times, one will clam up and the other one will blow up. There seems to be some areas where we can't meet in the middle and come to a compromise—especially when it comes to intimacy. Communication and consummation are connected to each other in life. The sun *does* go down on your anger, because you go to bed mad at your spouse who seems to be very uninterested and unaffectionate toward you. You don't talk about this before, during, or afterward; it has become *the* reason for so very many fights and tears through the years. You don't know what is wrong and what in the world has happened to your marriage or your mate. It influences the rest of your life together and sometimes, that confusion and anger comes out in other areas of married life. When you do try to talk together, one of you or both of you have some unwholesome talk. You feel like the other is not listening because they are just not improving—or touching or kissing or embracing like you used to when first married. Marriage can get so messy, so easily. Might you be in one of these marriages? Might one of you be going to bed angry—or lonely—while you try to fall asleep? Will you both talk about this topic? Will you talk with me or someone else on staff about it? Yes, every night, millions of couples go to sleep with the sun going down on their anger because one of you lies there feeling *so* frustrated and humiliated, rejected and resentful, disappointed and denied and deprived—while the other one is sleeping. This is how marriages fall apart.

JACOB WITH RACHEL AND LEAH: Genesis 29–30

What a memorable story, where Jacob worked all these years and ended up getting a different wife than he thought he was getting. What a surprise he had in store for him after waiting and working all those years! He thought he was getting Rachel but instead he got Leah. He got tricked and duped. He ended up married to someone he really didn't expect. There are lots of husbands or wives today who feel exactly like Jacob does here. They are so very surprised at the spouse they ended up with and they got something or someone very different than they ever dreamed. True? Certain personality traits or physical idiosyncrasies or behaviors come out that take you for a surprise. Just ask Jacob about his surprise! Each husband and wife here can probably think of different things on their lists that they didn't expect. I thought he was tidy but he sure isn't. I thought she liked to cook but now she doesn't. The list could go on. What are some of his or her qualities that make you surprised?

One quality that surprises and actually shocks a lot of couples is in the area of intimacy. We wonder what happened and who this person is—like Jacob thought! They used to be romantic and now they're not. They used to want to cuddle but now they don't. We used to be affectionate but now one of us doesn't seem interested. They used to show how much they desired us but now we're not sure. You feel like you ended up married to someone totally different, each new night. You want a refund maybe. One of you feels unloved, unwanted, and unattractive—you feel like Leah felt. Does anyone wonder how Leah did feel in this story? She must have felt so deeply hurt. She was now married to a man who didn't want to be married to her and showed it. He wanted nothing to do with her and showed it. Anyone sad for Leah here? I am. Do you feel her pain? Have you made your spouse feel like Leah felt here? He had no desire for her. It showed. Do you do that? Do you show affection anymore? Maybe you've become like Jacob and have someone else in your heart that you'd rather have? Maybe it's someone you see in an adult video, someone you see at work, someone who you see in the neighborhood? You're interested in someone else besides your spouse, like Jacob wanted Rachel and not Leah in our story.

Let's be real here: Who and how do you identify with in our story in Genesis? Do you feel like unloved Leah? Do you now feel like you're married to someone different than you dated? Do you wish you had a spouse who would show his or her love? Do you have a secret person who you would rather be married to, right now? Might you need to have a talk with God and ask Him to heal your heart or help you change? Do you need to share something with your spouse to open up new communication? Where might your marriage be in our story?

SPOUSES UNDERSTANDING EACH OTHER'S NEEDS: 1 Peter 3:7

We are told to be extremely wise and perceptive about our spouse's unique needs, weaknesses, and limitations as we closely study our partner to know how to best love them in ways that they value and appreciate the most. This is not that easy. The NIV version tell us to be considerate as we live with our spouses and to treat them with respect as the weaker partner. "Weaker" refers to their physical but not emotional or spiritual strength, because the next verse assures men and women of our equal status, being heirs together of the gracious gift of life.

God has much to teach us about love. You throw away whatever instruction manual you've been generally and previously taught on how to show your love to the opposite sex and your marriage mate. You learn to start from scratch and write a new manual that has to be customized with their name on it, none other. All that matters now is learning *your* spouse and what makes your spouse feel truly loved. For some, it's practical expressions of love around the house from your hands. For others, it's little expressions of thoughtful gifts from you to them. For others, it's verbal expressions of love from your mouth. For some, it's quiet expressions of togetherness from your schedule. For others, it's physical or sexual expressions of love from your body. Actually, it's all five and even more. However, which unique way does *your* spouse feel most loved? What makes them the happiest and feel most secure? What makes them glow? Do you really know? Our text tells us to have a deep understanding of their needs. None is superior or inferior to others. That includes sexual needs. Understanding each other in this text can and must include this part of your partner.

Sadly today for some reason, some spouses berate or belittle or just ignore this desire that their partner has for them alone. It's seen as less important or less spiritual. It's not. One spouse just stops showing romantic or sexual or physical gestures to the other spouse and they now starve. Our text tells us to meet the needs of our partner and go outside our boundaries. Understanding his or her sex drive is part of this understanding of your partner, too. Might you two have a talk about this verse and challenge today? Is it just possible that you're not as wise as you think or as willing as you think to meet your spouse's needs? You can show your spouse respect by showing him or her romance. Yes! God will give you that strength and wisdom when you ask Him and your spouse.

ABRAHAM / SARAH AND ISAAC / REBEKAH:
Genesis 20; 26

We read this story and wonder what was going through the head of both Abraham and Isaac in participating in actions which allowed their wives to be taken by other men, without defending them. We read that they were scared of losing their lives in the cruel cultures of their day. Did anyone stop to think about how Sarah and Rebekah might have felt here? Where is my husband? He promised to protect me and make me feel more secure. This is not what I wanted or planned. I am now in the bedroom of another man because of my husband. I feel so humiliated. I feel so unloved. I feel so alone. I have been deserted and abandoned. I feel so rejected and resentful tonight. Again, what was going through the head and felt in the heart by these women?

There are many women—and men—who feel the same way these women did. They wonder why their spouse seems to have deserted them and left them alone. Instead of being in the king's chambers, they feel like they're in their own death chambers and cry at night. Why won't my husband or wife be with me sexually? This is not the way it's supposed to be. They feel unloved and abandoned, just like Sarah and Rebekah felt. They should be laying here next to me and not elsewhere. Sometimes, the spouses aren't at home and sometimes, they're up watching TV or on the computer. One goes to bed without the other, just like in our story here. Husbands or wives, do you identify with Abraham or Isaac in this story? You might think you have a great reason for what you're doing, but did you wonder how your spouse feels as you aren't there *or* as you're there but you don't kiss them good-night *or* show them marital affection anymore? Your spouse feels as equally deserted as these spouses in this story.

Might you instead identify here with Sarah or Rebekah? Do you see yourself in them or in their marriage of silence or absence? May this story move you to break down, confess, or grieve—depending on which person describes you here? Did you ever stop to think that your spouse lays awake at night so disappointed? Do you see the consequences of your lack of attention or affection not shown? Might you need to talk together to see if one of you happens to emotionally feel so deserted and alone, like these Bible women did in Genesis?

JOSEPH SAYING NO TO ANOTHER'S SEXUAL ADVANCES: Genesis 39

We applaud and approve of Joseph refusing the advances of a married woman. This is one of the most well-known stories in the Bible and used in a lot of messages about premarital or extramarital sexual activity. We hold him up as the example, especially in his reasons given. Let's change this scenario in just one small detail. Let's say that this was his wife who was requesting the exact same thing of him! Forget about it being Potiphar's wife and let's assume it was his wife asking here. It changes everything, doesn't it? What would have been the best response then? Saying "no" to the sexual advances of someone else's wife is a good thing. Saying "no" to the sexual advances of your own wife—or husband—is not a good thing. Every day and night, we see spouses unfortunately saying what Joseph said—but instead to their own spouses. They have some reason, or they give no reason. They say "no." Their spouses feel rejected, unattractive, and undesired. It hurts them deeply.

God knows how important it is for a husband and wife to say "yes" to each other. Instead, He says we should not deprive the other since our bodies belongs to them. There are many Josephs saying "no" to their spouses when they should say "yes." Might you be one of them? I'm glad you are saying "no" to the advances of another, but I hope you are saying "yes" to the request for sexual affection from your spouse. It all depends on who is asking, doesn't it? "Yes" said to only one but "yes" should be said frequently to one, the one God gave to you so that you would not want to say "yes" to another. God knows how tempted we can be and how important it is for a couple to come together so that they will not fall apart. Be that wise and wonderful Joseph and definitely say "no" to others who request your physical affection . . . but make sure you are saying "yes" to your spouse who is requesting affection. Joseph's words of "How can I do this and sin against my God?" could be modified and applied to you in your saying "How can I *not* do this and sin against my God?" God commands us to take care of the emotional and sexual needs of our spouses. Not doing that is equally wrong.

May we go one step further and apply this today? How about these similar but different words that I ask you to consider when you are reluctant or resistant to express that unique sexual bond you should have with them: How can you do this and tempt your spouse to also sin against God" Let's take this story of Joseph and apply his words to our marriage relationship.

PAUL'S DESIRING TIMOTHY'S PRESENCE BECAUSE HE WAS DESERTED BY DEMAS AND EVERYONE ELSE: 2 Timothy 4:9–22

Strong apostle Paul, who defied kings and endured persecution, is at the end of his life and now he knows it. He sits in prison, and we get to see the God-inspired words used to describe some of his emotional feelings. What a glimpse into his thoughts here in 1 and 2 Timothy. He's asking Timothy to hurry up and come see him. Paul seems lonely and it's nice to know his feelings are normal, and again, inspired by God to also put in the Bible. He is the One who said that it is not good for people to be alone, remember that? Paul is at the place where he wants and needs someone's physical presence, emotional company, and spiritual support. There is not a thing wrong with this feeling and nowhere is Paul described as weak for needing another human being. Others deserted him and abandoned him. They just left him and left him forever. He mentions it. It surprised and disappointed him and he doesn't mind saying it. He is not complaining or sinning in telling the raw truth that someone dear to him has also deserted him. Demas previously ministered to folks, alongside of Paul. Yes, we're told that the Lord stood by Paul's side and gave him new strength, but we're also told how people who were once dear to him had now also deserted him.

Do you have a Demas in your life? Might it be a prodigal child or even a distant spouse? Might it be a past friend who now isn't? Does your husband or wife feel like a Demas because they seem to have deserted you in your time of deep need? Maybe that need is at night time when you wish you had your spouse's company or cuddling? What happened? You ministered together like Paul and Demas but now, he or she has deserted you in terms of showing physical or sexual affection and companionship. You can be honest here; Paul was. Yes, God stands by your side but it still hurts that your mate does not. Nor does he or she seem to lay next to you anymore. He wasn't wrong to share how sad he was now. Might you need to share this loneliness and bewilderment with your Demas today? Let's go a step further. Are you being a Demas who has deserted someone who now misses you? We're told that Demas loved this present world, and that's the reason given. What is your reason? Do you love someone else? Your job? Your computer?

Your children? What has taken the place of your spouse? Why do you deprive your spouse of your presence, your body, your physical bonding, and your becoming one flesh? Paul needed Timothy to visit him. Does your wife or husband need you as well? It's what you vowed to each other, to have and to hold, until death do you part. There are so many marriages where one feels the other has simply deserted him or her. It's because these spouses have—when it comes to emotional, physical, or spiritual oneness. Don't wait for the news of this desertion and divorce to hit the pages of Scripture or divorce court. Do something about it today. Renew your vows to your spouse.

Additional and advanced studies in the Scriptures on the topic of marital sexual reluctance

Temptation is often discussed in the Scriptures. We're usually told that the world or Satan are the real reasons for temptation (Job 1–2; Luke 4:1–14; 1 Peter 5:8–9) but we often forget that we can actually be partial reasons for making other people stumble and fall (Rom. 14–15). In 1 Corinthians 7:5, we're also told that Satan uses marital sexual deprival as a way in which we can tempt spouses to sin. Whenever you preach on temptation, don't forget to include this one in your list!

Your body now belongs to God when you become a believer (1 Cor. 3:16–17; 6:19–20), and it now also belongs to your spouse when you get married!

First Corinthians 7:4 lets a husband and wife know that they gave up rights to their bodies that they used to have. They now belongs to their spouses; this is a huge change that must be taught in our churches, in every message we preach about our bodies, in whatever setting. Knowing your body belongs to your spouse is one of the very first theological tools you need to know to help you avoid sexually depriving him or her. Your soul and your body are now gifts you give your spouse in an act of worship.

Selflessness and sacrifice—where we treat others better than ourselves and put their needs above our needs (Phil. 2:1–18) in imitating Christ Himself. Selfishness has no place in the life of a Christian and this includes sex in marriage. It is an attitude of giving and serving, humbling and obeying—just like Jesus did. When the right Christ-like attitude exists, the actions easily or naturally follow. Extend your messages on service or servant leadership toward putting your spouse's needs first and foremost above your own. We don't withhold our bodies—we give them to our spouse in physical oneness. This is the foundation that directs how we approach the Christian life and marriage as well. You can even preach about the selfishness of marital sexual deprival when you're discussing the humility of Jesus.

Keeping the marriage bed pure (Heb. 13:4) can be easily accomplished by not allowing bitterness to grow up to cause trouble and defile (Heb. 12:15). I don't think it's a coincidence that these verses are so close in proximity and practicality. God knows how easily bitterness makes bedtime torture for either one or both spouses. Bitterness and bedroom behavior are related.

Unconditional love is expressed to us in that while we were still sinners, Christ died for us (Rom. 5:8). I find this a great text to use in helping couples to see that we are to show that same kind of love to our spouses, regardless of moods. While we're yet sinners, our spouse continues to love us and serve us. Period.

While they're yet sinners, we don't withhold love or expressions of love from them, no matter what they're doing. Our love and our body is a gift and not a reward. While they are at their worst, we're supposed to show love to them at our best. While we were at our worst, God showed His love to us and gave us His very best.

Grace—and marital sex—are unconditionally given and not conditionally earned. While we were yet sinners, we were still loved. Go and do likewise to your spouse.

Celibacy is a hot topic in our churches. Whenever you talk about it, could you please mention that marriage is *not* the place to practice this celibacy. Just the opposite is true. Again, biblical balance is our goal. God has given both messages and not just one in the Bible. You have been given the green light and no longer have the red light. Enjoy it! Make sure you shout this from the rooftops. *Don't just condemn premarital or extramarital sexual activity without celebrating marital sexual activity in the very same message or sentence.* Too many marriages have involuntary eunuchs and marital celibacy, which are not what God ever intended. God is serious about sex being a vital and vibrant part of our marriage as long as humanly possible. Let's preach that positive message, too.

PREPARING FOR YOUR FUTURE

12

MY CHALLENGE TO THE CHURCH OF THE FUTURE

There were once men "from Issachar, men who understood the times and knew what Israel should do. . . ."

—1 Chronicles 12:32

Today's and tomorrow's church needs more men and women of Issachar who wisely understand the times and know exactly what the church should next do. Many of the people in our churches and communities to whom we are called to minister are either sexually wounded or sexually addicted, broken, or confused. Depending on the size of your church, they will range from a handful to hundreds. When you count up the types of sexual topics we've shared in this book, it's a good chance that their total numbers might reach in the thousands, for some churches. They are haunted by memories, seduced by temptation, and shunned by church. These *are* the times in which we live, and we desperately need good leadership.

Unfortunately, *we have far too many old-fashioned Methuselahs who are leading the church, when we really need more cutting-edge Issachars!* We must equip church leaders who are able to work in a Corinthian, not a Victorian, society.

Let's not pretend any longer. Let's not long for the good ol' days of the past. We must be contemporary, compassionate, competent, and conservative at the same time—filled with truth and grace. A huge cataclysmic cultural shift has happened and we must have missed it. We seem to have our heads stuck in the sand, unaware of what happened. But, it is not too late. It's never too late with God.

I offer these solutions and directions to the church of the future:

1. *I challenge today's Christian colleges, universities, and seminaries to better prepare our church leaders to minister to the millions who are part of a sexually scarred generation.* They must offer intensive training in the specific areas of sexual sins and wounds. Seminary courses must equip future leaders and pastors to effectively preach to and counsel with the victims of the sexual revolution. Seminaries who claim to be preparing leaders to minister to today's culture had better have a curriculum that includes the topic of sex; otherwise, their claims and advertising are totally false. *Bible colleges and seminaries who publicly boast that they are on the "cutting edge of ministry" but are silent about sex are lying to the world and are also doing injustice to their students in not preparing them for ministry in today's society.* Seminaries must get out of the small little box they now live in and get us ready.

   Review their current curricula, and you'll likely find that there is nothing whatsoever about sex. Do you see anything there about specific issues that are addressed in this book? How much longer do we have to wait for them to finally get with the program? This can no longer be ignored. They must bring in professionals and ministries who are biblically grounded and currently working with all different types of sexually wounded or addicted people. Take advice from those on the battlefield.

And for those of you considering entering the pastoral ministry, why not consider a future in Christian counseling instead? Could that be your calling? There is a lifetime's worth of needy people with sexual problems that you can help. Would you rather help people one-on-one? Might that be a better fit for you?

2. *I call upon leaders who produce Christian literature, curricula, films, songs, and books to reach a very sexually saturated culture.* We must use every communication method and medium to teach God's Word. No longer can we be satisfied with the same old simplistic message of "just say no." Tell them what "just saying yes" has done to people who are now suffering in silence or incarcerated in prison. Let them tell their stories as well. Make materials for *all* ages on this. Get realistic and get creative. *In addition to telling them to "wait until marriage"—tell the stories of the vast majority who did NOT wait, and tell the stories of those who didn't have a choice in waiting but whose choice was abruptly taken away from them.*

Make books, CDs, and songs about what pornography did to a strong family. Tell the story of a church who helped a family whose daughter got pregnant. Share the testimony of an adult woman who experienced being molested as a child and yet was emotionally healed by internalizing and memorizing the Scriptures. Show the many mistakes that people make in counseling a rape victim and how Christians can avoid these mistakes. Make us better; make us experts. Make a film or song about a husband and wife physically delighting in each other's bodies on their honeymoon night. Show the pain of sexual refusal. Tastefully re-create the Song of Solomon. Tell the stories of ex-homosexuals who came to Christ and how their lives were both gradually and drastically changed. Design a quarterly Sunday School course on the sexual topics in Proverbs 5 through 7. The list is endless. Get bolder and better as you speak to today's generation.

Make powerful and practical Christian education materials, films, tracts, and songs about some of the biblical characters, fascinating stories, and sexual lessons that you have learned from this book. Each of these sermons could be expanded. Create intensive educational materials on our bodies made in God's image, the male and female sexes as equal before God, self-control, sexual temptation, sexual intercourse, forgiveness, singleness, our new power in Christ, overcoming sinful habits, our merciful and compassionate God, and ministering in practical ways to sexually hurt people. The list is again almost endless. Reach this culture for Christ. Let's scratch people where they itch, and stop riding denominational or theological hobbyhorses that trod over those who have fallen on the battlefield!

3. *I challenge the future church to have better family, children's, youth, marriage, and singles ministries.* Church members and attenders have sexual temptations and dark wounds that are not bandaged by our antiquated and shallow models of "family ministries." I am talking about providing more than crafts for the children, bowling for the teens, and movies for the singles. A five-minute weekly children's sermon is no match for the hundreds of hours of sexual content they see every week. The church needs after-school programs to compete for this time when Internet dangers abound for those who are just not supervised. *The time has come when children will not only love puppets but now they actually need puppets—to tell us how and where they were sexually fondled by adults.*

Today's singles need a ton of weekend events to take their mind off weekend temptations. They are waiting so much longer to get married and are exposing themselves to much more temptation and at a much earlier age than ever before. The church needs to plan ministries for ten to twenty years of continual sexual conversation and temptation before people get married in our churches. We have a younger generation who will best be served by a shepherd who watches over their souls, not just a jock who works out their bodies and occupies their time. Today's youth need a pastoral and not just a recreational leader. *It's about time churches started paying to hire theologically trained men and women to minister to their children and youth.* The average church volunteer in charge of these vital ministries will not know enough to address the tough and touchy topics, like sex. What will your current youth pastor say to the fifteen-year-old girl who was raped by her date at her high school prom? What will be said to the eighteen-year-old teen who has masturbated to hundreds of pornographic movies? What will he or she say to the teenage girl who had an abortion and now is scared to death that she will be sterile for the rest of her life—or that God is punishing her for her abortion? What will you say to the little boy who was sodomized and gang-raped by older boys in the woods near his house? Does your children's-church worker know how to get the eight-year-old girl to talk about her stepfather who penetrated her last night?

I also want clean teens and singles to be involved in Sunday worship services. We have to help boys and girls to see the opposite sex as spiritual creatures and not just physical objects. Boys and girls, teens and singles, all need to know that there are godly yet good-looking members of the opposite sex. Church can help.

4. *I challenge churches to develop small groups where people can share their sexual trauma and failures in confidential but compassionate settings.* We have support groups for alcoholism, weight loss, and divorce—so why not for the sexually hurting? Imagine the fifty to seventy-five percent of the church who will personally and immediately benefit here. Often, I advocate same-sex groups to facilitate more support. Ladies need to share with ladies, and men need to get help from other men. Support groups dealing with a specific sexual wound or temptation should be freshly created and publicized within your church—after you've taken the necessary steps we have already outlined in the beginning of our book. They need to find a good Christian friend, like David had in Jonathan. They need to get things off their chest. They need to lay their burdens down and build their strength up. *Small groups like these, properly supervised, will ease the avalanche of counseling requests that will hopefully be coming from your brand-new and improved style of preaching now.* One Sunday morning in the future, ask your church members to go to your website

or write down the name of a person in the church that they would go to with personal issues. Train them specifically in sexual issues to be a core group of counselors who represent the church. They are the people you can start with. Give them this book to study closely, so that they will be much better equipped!

5. *People who minister to sexually tempted and traumatized people must frequently hold themselves accountable to others.* They need their own support group to give them fresh insights as to their own preaching practices, counseling situations, and sexual temptations they will now encounter. Share with others the precise sexual wording you intend to use this Sunday. See what they say or advise instead. Fellow local pastors should all be on the same page, praying for each other. Iron sharpens iron. Why not get a local group of fellow pastors to all work on a sermon together that collectively and carefully inserts your thoughts, sentences, or paragraphs about a sexual topic? You can have more freedom if you all decide to swap churches, so that you can feel more freedom in preaching next Sunday. You might all be amazed, and you can all be videotaped and compare notes. They must also hold themselves accountable to their own spouses who will, understandably, be prone to worry much more now. They know of other pastors who gradually slipped, fell into temptation, lost their church and family. Talk to your spouse about nearly everything you experience. Do make sure that you believe in your innermost heart that your spouse is the *only* one on earth that God has ordained for your body to enjoy.

6. *Pastors need to ask about the sexual history and behavior of people they minister to during any and all kinds of counseling situations today.* You need to broaden your horizons as to the real reasons behind some personal or marriage problems. Whether it be personal, premarital, or marriage counseling: You need to bring up the topic of sex more frequently than you now do. Chances are that you are forgetting to delve into this neglected area that just might point to the answer or key you are looking for. *Pastors often get stumped at discerning what the problem*

*or solution really is, because they do not ever ask about
sex.* More often than you realize, the solution to people's
needs or problems lies in the sexual arena of their lives.
The examples are endless as to how something sexual that
was done to them, or is being done by them, is now af-
fecting them on the deepest level right now without their
realizing it. You will be amazed at how quickly you get to
the real root of a problem without beating around the bush
forever. You will be astonished at how people open up to
share sexual secrets, but they will do so only when you
specifically ask and make it easier for them to share. They
will rarely volunteer or initiate such information on their
own. You'll be so excited at the relief you bring to people
that they can finally share this hurt. Gently open up this
wound with wisdom. Don't sound judgmental at their answers. Your improved preaching style lets them know you
are now approachable and discerning.

Especially as it relates to premarital counseling sessions,
you must ask. Ask about their desires for their honeymoon
night and sexual intimacy together. Ask about their sexual
virginity or history as individuals and as a couple. Ask who
is more experienced and how many sexual partners each
has had in the past. Ask about AIDS testing. Ask about
all seven sexual topics in this book, not just the one about
their premarital sexual activity or virginity. Let's not be
naive, and let's give them the opportunity to finally bring it
up! Ask about incest, molestation, rape, abortion, pornography, homosexual or heterosexual temptations. *Assume
the worst, not the best.* Probe into their frequently visited
websites, reading, viewing, or weekend habits. Tell them
that you ask everybody, not just them.

Probe, delve, inquire, explore, expose—but do it with
gentleness and mercy, not with harshness or wrath. It took
a lot of guts for them to finally come to you. *You don't
have to prove how spiritual you are by expressing shock
and anger at their sexual behavior. They have already heard
your previous sermons and know this.*

7. *Consider upgrading your staff with a full-time biblical
counselor or center that can handle a wider range of people's sexual hurts and needs.* Of course, this assumes that

seminaries and parachurch ministries are training these types of leaders. Your people are now spending their time and money going to the world for help. You help them in every area of life but sexuality. Why is this area of life excluded? Why not have your own Christian counseling center, or hired staff, as an extended ministry to your local community? How cool would that be?

I would like to propose that the contemporary church create a new staff position called "Minister of Hurts and Habits." It would be wise to encompass the widest range of ages and genders in the church while specializing in emotional and spiritual healing and wholeness of God's people. What a great idea to consider as you grow your church! Give people an alternative option and give them the right solutions from God. Have biblically trained counselors for the sexual issues mentioned in this book. At least seek out the local parachurch specialized ministries who have expertise in any of these seven sexual book topics, to help you do a better job. Financially support them or intellectually learn from them.

The church of the twenty-first century will also need to be experts in treating sexual dysfunction. With the increase of sexual abuse, incest, rape, premarital sin, homosexual sin, abortion, and pornography—men and women feel very dirty, angry, inadequate, cold, fearful, and ashamed to have sexual relations with their mates in marriage. Sexual reluctance and refusal just might be happening due to these.

8. *The contemporary church needs to budget more funds to effectively minister to the sexually troubled people in their community.* Do you really need to paint the church sanctuary, again? What about giving some of that money to the family whose nineteen-year-old college daughter was raped and needs hospital care for the baby she has wisely chosen not to abort? Millions of pregnant women choose abortion for financial reasons, when the church could help them with the medical expenses of carrying their babies to full term. Practice what you preach, especially for those who believe in covenant theology. Do you really need that fancy technology when you can use the money to help a mother and daughter's living expenses while her husband is in jail

for sexual-misconduct charges? Will you financially help the wife, and children, of the man who has abandoned them to live out his life as an openly gay man, since it has become much more acceptable now? Who will help pay for the counseling expenses for a little child in your church whose stepfather has been molesting her for years? *Must your church spend thousands of dollars on newer chairs when they could give it to a local ministry helping homosexuals find Jesus?*

Do you want the money from your most generous building-fund supporter, even though it is acquired by sexual practices that are not biblical? Do you know if they have income from doing abortions or producing sexually explicit materials today? What about giving financial support to Christian lawyers who represent women who had abortions and are now suing the hospitals for medical malpractice? Ever consider donating money to ministries who try to lobby the state legislature to make or amend laws to biblical standards of sexuality? What about the church who is helping a family in transition because they recently gave up their profitable Internet sex business and are both now looking for new jobs as a result of their recent conversion to Christ? How would your church leaders react to these ideas? Our concept of missions must change and become more realistic today. Will your church actually put their money where your mouth hopefully is?

9. *Malpractice insurance and pastoral confidentiality are topics to consider if you're getting involved in the sexual healing of individuals.* Ours is a litigious society and the church is not immune from this. Catholic and Protestant traditions will always differ yet still wrestle with the legal reporting of confessed illegal sexual crimes and behaviors. It's mandatory, and should really be a non-issue. This is not an easy topic today. In addition to knowing the phone numbers of your church members, do you need to memorize the numbers to your local state agencies or police station? And will people in your church or community come to you for sexual counseling if they know you will have to call the police? Will you be arrested if you don't report? Should they pack before they come? Should you pack before you

counsel? Will you be in trouble for not reporting a middle-aged man who was arrested last week but had previously shared with you that he was sexually attracted to younger boys? When do you report? Based on temptation alone? How strong does that temptation have to be and how do you tell when it reaches a danger level? A family whose homosexual son commits suicide later finds out that you told him that his lifestyle was sinful. They fully blame you for his emotional depression and you're now involved in legal entanglements.

You tell the wife of a man who contracted AIDS through adulterous affairs and he sues you for breaking local confidentiality laws. Do your leaders want you to tell them about the man who confesses to homosexual temptation yet wants to go on the upcoming men's retreat? Do you tell the civil authorities about a man sharing with you his sexual temptations toward young children as a result of his pornography? Do you or don't you tell the parents of a teen who tells her youth leader about her abortion last month? A middle-aged man admits to doing something that sounds like rape as he unburdens his soul and cries to God and you; what do you do?

Once again, the list is almost endless. Let's talk about these issues finally.

10. *Sooner or later, the church will need to locally and globally talk about AIDS and other sexually transmitted diseases.* Spouting off a bunch of Bible verses about adultery, premarital sex, and homosexuality is just not good enough any longer. It is not that cut-and-dried. What about children sexually molested by an AIDS carrier? Do you tell your nursery workers about the new AIDS baby there? Is their birth not ordained by God? Are they of any less value in God's eyes? What about the woman raped at work by an AIDS carrier? What about the deacon who now has AIDS because of his wife's one-night stand? What about the possibility of the faithful and innocent partner getting AIDS if they remain married to their now-infected spouse? Do we tell them just to forgive and forget? Turning the other cheek isn't much comfort or wisdom. We need more.

11. *Church discipline is another emerging topic for discussion in the church that is attempting to minister to a sexually active generation.* To most churches this is a foreign language and is never considered today. Some churches are quite selective, chauvinistic, and inconsistent in application. Remember that the purpose of church discipline is to restore, not just rebuke (Gal. 6:1). Denominational disciplinary boards should have people who read this book as their shepherds, not just a bunch of seasoned pastors of larger churches. This sexual arena is not for the faint of heart nor for the amateurs. Consider before you condemn; delve before you discipline.

A young lady gets pregnant and some church leaders start talking of discipline. What about the other girls and guys who are sleeping around but just did not happen to get caught or pregnant? One of your members goes to gay clubs and there is discussion of discipline—but what about other church members whose weekends are filled with casual sex at college activities? Know of those?

One of your church members is a doctor who performs abortions and is asked to reconsider. What about the nurses in your congregation who assist here? What about your generous church donor who happens to be the pharmaceutical CEO whose company produces abortion pills? Are we being consistent?

A married woman has an affair and does not want to end it, and the church leaders want to talk with her. Do they know she is tired of her husband who insists she perform painful and perverted sexual acts with him, while being forced to watch pornography with him? Will they equally talk to him or ignore that?

Church members want to picket the local pornography store, but what about doing the same with the local high school that teaches teens how to have sex?

Do you know that the homosexual man in your singles group now hates women because he was forced to have sex with his mother, who is also a prominent church member? What will you say to each or both of them?

Instead of privately or publicly chastising a sexually active young woman, might you equally consider her father, who taught her all she knows from pornographic magazines and movies? Or will you chat with the boys in the youth group who seduced her at summer youth camp? Or her school counselor (and your church member) who gives her all the condoms she needs? Or her doctor (and your church member) who performed her abortion without parental consent?

I am asking today's church to be thoroughly fair and consistent, as well as perceptive, when it comes to the causes and expressions of sexual pain and grief. Not all people commit sexual sin for hedonistic, sensual reasons. Most people are overreacting to earlier anger, neglect, abuse, hurt, confusion, betrayal, and scars.

Sinners cause other sinners to stumble; let's not be too quick to condemn.

One sexual sin that appears to be quite small and done in secret often causes someone else a lifetime of pain and causes a ripple effect where the one who was wounded, now wounds others. We must try to stop the generational and harmful cycle that has been set in motion by a single sexual sin.

12. *The church of the future must emphasize babies in the twenty-first century.* We have raised a generation of "condom kids," in which the worst and last things they ever want in life is a disease—or an unwanted pregnancy. The two have been unfairly put in the same category. How sad but true. America does *not* love children any longer. We are told to do whatever it takes to avoid pregnancy, at all costs. Teens are told that having a child and then raising a child is the last thing on earth that you ever want to do. You've been trained for dozens of years by the time you reach adulthood, and that doesn't go away overnight. The church has to make a strategic and determined effort to uplift babies and children. Make a big deal over the birth or baptism of every baby in your church. Show support for your nursery workers, vacation Bible school, and children's staff.

Tell your people to be on the lookout for pregnant women who aren't sure if they want to raise a child, and match them up with Christian couples who will. Tell that to the local school counselors, youth group, singles group, dorm supervisors, military chaplains, abortion clinics, and crisis-pregnancy centers. Put up signs in public places—let everyone know that your church loves babies and children of all colors and sizes. Jesus loved children; let's do what He did.

13. *I challenge the church to be much more careful and biblical in our topics of submission, forgiveness, grief, headship, and especially anger.* As a result of reading this book, I hope that you more fully understand the very complicated and hidden painful reasons why some people do what they have done. In the past, you would have had little compassion and competence with certain types of people who committed certain sexual behaviors. Now you know that things are not always as they appear to be. There are painful pasts you just didn't know about or care to ask about. There are a lot of things you don't know about when it comes to the past of this person. This does not excuse their behavior but it does help explain it. There are understandable (though not justifiable) reasons for their behavior. You've gotten smarter and nicer, hopefully, as a result of your reading. You've changed and grown to appreciate the need for truth and grace.

Not only do I want you to extend Christian forgiveness and compassion to them—but I also want you to think twice before you demand it from them.

I counseled a lady who had been traded sexually to the landlord in exchange for the rent, since the age of eight. They had little money since her dad passed away unexpectedly without any life insurance. Mom learned how lucrative and profitable her daughter's body was and ultimately rented her out to other men in the neighborhood, who would in turn bring their friends. This went on for ten years. Finally, this girl felt so helpless that she tried to kill herself to escape all the pain. It did not work and her mom finally realized she should stop. She did. Eventually, this little girl grew up and got married and was converted to Christ as an adult. She had forgotten all her past, she thought, until she had her first baby. All those ten years of childhood sexual memories came back quite vividly.

At the age of twenty-eight, she confronted her mom about her behavior and her mom quickly replied, "Well, you wanted it. It was your fault." Mother denied any responsibility, and placed all the blame and shame on her daughter. Imagine accusing and blaming your eight-year-old daughter for sexual acts like these. The twenty-eight-year-old daughter went into a very severe depression and was admitted to a mental institution just a few days after she had spoken to her mother.

Now I ask you this: Are you going to put more blame and shame on this young lady for not instantly and easily forgiving her mother, and for feeling so hostile and angry toward her now? Most people and pastors do exactly that as they counsel. Talk about pouring salt on wounds. Talk about dull insensitivity and bad timing. We have this thing about *instantly* demanding forgiveness from wounded people.

I counseled a Christian woman who became sexually involved with a man who promised to marry her—that is, until she became pregnant. He gave her a choice: Have the baby and lose him, *or* have him and lose the baby. She chose him and yes, she chose abortion. In a couple of weeks, he left her for other conquests.

For six long years, she tried to get him back. Somehow that would justify her decision and soothe her loss. She did not want to admit that she killed her infant for someone who lied to her and left her. She lost everything that was near or dear to her. She feels totally deceived and discarded, for she was.

Are you going to quickly and glibly tell her to forgive him when he has never asked for forgiveness or admitted he did anything wrong? When she stands next to him singing in the choir, will you counsel her to just forget about and forgive him for the past? Is it really that easy for her to just get on with her life, that easily and quickly? In our effort to help people, we unwisely expect the impossible. We just have to be patient and let God speak to hearts in terms of timing here.

The list is almost endless and hopefully you see the main point being made. *There is an enormous amount of rage, bitterness, devastation, pain, depression, confusion, and anger in people who have been sexually hurt.* It will not go away overnight or with a simple prayer, sermon, Bible verse, or counseling session. It hurts—and all hurts, whether they be physical or emotional, happen to take time to heal. Too often, the church squashes and suppresses anger and tells us never to be angry. Are we supposed to simply and instantly and easily forgive and forget—regardless of the offender who has never apologized to us? I cringe when I hear such simplistic and guilt-inducing words, especially from pastors and believers. There are thousands of stories similar to those above. Yes, I know that forgiveness is necessary. Sooner or later, it *must* be practiced. You can't hold grudges. Bitterness is a sin we should avoid. But please, give people some time. Trust God to do *His* job. Don't make them feel even worse again by laying extra burdens and false guilt on their souls and shoulders. Don't ask them to do something so difficult, so quickly, so casually and thus, callously. Have the person work through this very deep anger and gradually forgive the offending party. But don't insist they do it now or never. As a result, you only launch them into deeper depression. Jesus came to make us free, not frozen.

So be careful whenever you preach or talk about forgiveness and anger, and remember that there are people who have a pretty good reason to be angry. In this fallen world of selfish sinners, it is to be expected that people will be hurt by other people. In this fallen world of sexual sinners, it is to be fully expected that people will be wounded by people who will sexually abuse and discard them. We can even get wounded by our spouse in depriving us sexually. It's also to be fully expected that people will use such sadness or their situation as a crutch or excuse for inappropriate behavior in the future. Some people will want to cling to an unpleasant past mistreatment as an excuse for unbiblical behavior in the present. We shouldn't be surprised; look at Adam and Eve in the Garden of Eden. It is our job to equip people to gradually be able to deal with life's tragedies, by personally experiencing God's renewing grace and strength in life.

Submission is another biblical topic that has to be more carefully explored and explained in our churches. Women and children have been sold a false bill of goods about what submission is, and they are now paying the price of imbalance.

Submission does *not* mean that a man can do what he wants to a woman. Submission does *not* mean a father can do what he wants to his young child. Submission does *not* mean that you obey whatever a man (or an adult) tells you to believe or do. People will continue to use "submission" as a cloak for their evil. Our sinful nature will inevitable try to demand submission from those we view as powerless. We must carefully teach the complete truth on this crucial topic. Otherwise, sexual assault and abuse will continue to run rampant in our society. Every child and woman needs to know they *must* protect themselves from evil and speak out against it, even if it's found within their close friends, church, or family. There is no safe place except heaven. Let's face that fact. People of all genders and ages must confront and expose the evil deeds of others. Children today have to be occasionally asked if anyone has touched them in their private places, since a molester will tell them not to tell anyone about this. Adolescents and women need to be often asked if they were sexually forced against their will from any male friend. They need to be taught that this is *not* submission. We have to teach the whole counsel of God as to what submission doesn't mean. Most churches are not as advanced in this topic as they think.

14. *Same-sex attraction is a topic that is never going away in the church.* With Supreme Court decision legislation mandating same-sex marriages in the USA, it is now absolutely necessary that church leaders know their stuff on this. I think you already know my perspective from a previous chapter; I did my research and hope you will do yours. Have you? This is *the* huge tsunami for the future church and it's going to divide or unite your church, like no other issue has. Be prepared to help counsel the wife whose husband left her to embrace the gay lifestyle he kept secret for so long. Do you know what to say to her to help her regain her self-dignity? Are we prepared to serve and minister to the children of gay marriage, who don't know which one to call their mother or father?

Civil disobedience is a related topic that comes on the heels of this; it's another topic that churches will have to wrestle with as a result of same-sex legislation. This is a nightmare that is not going to go away while the church sticks its head in the sand, waiting for Jesus' return. The church might need reserve funds to get their pastor out of jail in the future.

That was the purpose of this book: to equip you to better communicate the Word of God—by becoming far more competent and compassionate toward those who have experienced sexual hurt, and to those who have inflicted sexual hurt.

This is your audience. These are the types of people God has given to you in your high and holy calling. This is the precise generation that God has called you to serve. King David, the man after God's own heart, was once described as having "served God's purpose in his own generation" (Acts 13:36).

Will you do the same? This is God's purpose and this is your generation. In a world that constructs their entire worldview and theology about sexuality from either the peer pressure of being pro-choice or from the people they know who happen to be gay, let's get ours from the pages of Scripture instead. Let's combine our therapeutic preaching with theological preaching. We must have both today. As Henry David Thoreau once said, "There are a thousand hacking at the branches of evil compared to the one who is striking at the root." I hope this book will help you begin to strike at the root and bring healing.

The world knows the problem but not the solution. The church knows the solution but not the problem.

Hopefully, no longer. . . .

It's our turn to be the experts on sex!

You're now better prepared and filled with truth and grace—both—as you engage a world that will continue to defy God but desperately need our God. Like God described in Jeremiah 2:13, they have forsaken Him—the spring of living waters—and they have dug their own broken cisterns which cannot hold water. Why would we be surprised at sexual sin or pain? God isn't. He predicted this all along. He also equipped us to tell them about the One who said in John 4:14 that "whoever drinks the water I give them will never thirst. Indeed, the water I give them will become in them a spring of water welling up to eternal life." Let's remind people that our God has visited earth in the person of Jesus Christ who has tenderly invited us to come to Him when we are weary and burdened. It is the Evil One who intends to destroy and steal, and Satan has done exactly that. He steals our joy, our freedom, our dignity, our confidence, and even our very souls. In stark contrast, Jesus is the One who came to give life and give it more abundantly. He is not the bad guy that people make God out to be. Just the opposite is true. May you feel afresh the anointing and calling from Isaiah 61:1 and again exclaim: "The Spirit of the Sovereign LORD is on me, because the LORD has anointed me to proclaim good news to the poor. He has sent me to bind up the brokenhearted, to proclaim freedom for the captives and release from darkness for the prisoners." This is the glorious gospel to which we've been entrusted to preach. Will you be like the Sadducees and the Pharisees who offered no help—*or* will you instead be the Good Samaritan when it comes to helping those who have been sexually robbed and beaten up in life? Let's show people that our solution is the Son who sets people free with the truth that also sets us free, indeed.